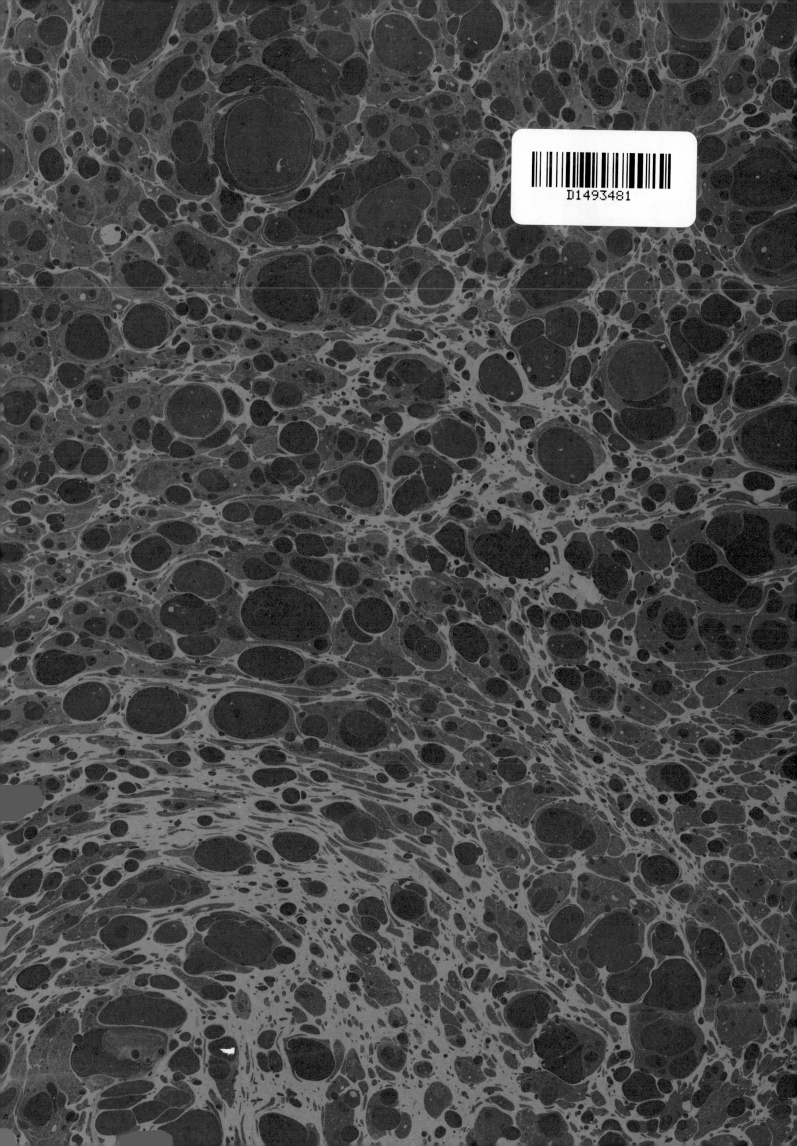

The Enchanted World

WATER SPIRITS

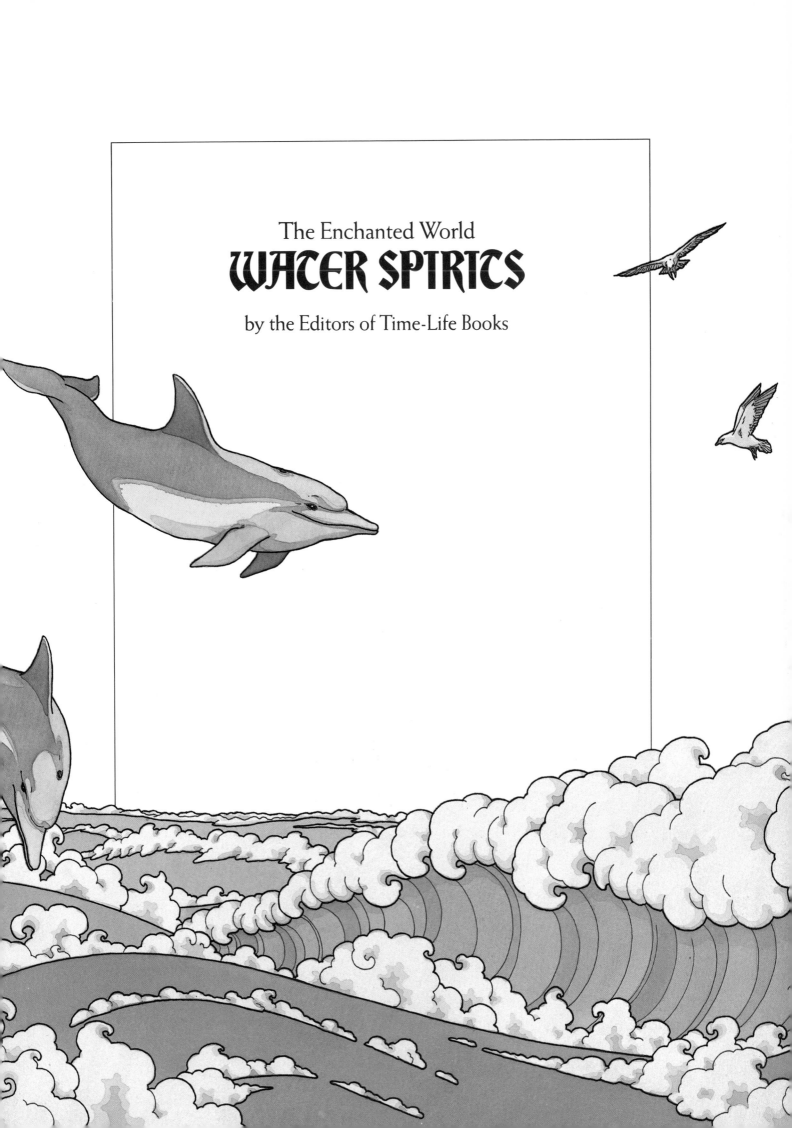

The Enchanted World

WATER SPIRITS

by the Editors of Time-Life Books

The Content

Time-Life Books · Amsterdam

Chapter One

A Wellspring of the Universe

Along Cornwall's stern south coast, where the land knots up into granite fists and finally surrenders to the battering waves of the sea, generations of fisherfolk once combed the shores for shipwrecked treasures. These wreckers profited by the gales that howled up the English Channel, dashing wooden trading vessels to splinters on the Cornish rocks. For days after a storm, fragments of the ships and the goods they carried—barrels of rum and salted beef, bales of flax, brass fittings on pieces of wreckage—washed up with the tides. The villagers who found these fruits of tragedy regarded them as gifts from the sea, like the catches of pilchard and mackerel that swelled their nets on good days. It seemed that, for every life the water took, it gave a living to another.

But to one Cornishman, the sea gave much more. A man of middle years named Lutey, he lived quietly with his wife and dog in a squat stone cottage at Cury, near Lizard Point. With his children grown and gone now, wrecking was the special pleasure of his idle hours. A thick ship's rudder made his mantlepiece, and on it sat a fine brass clock. In the corner, a gilded figurehead stared out over the earth-floored room with blank wooden eyes.

Lutey's life changed on a hazy spring afternoon, a day when bluish mists rose off the sea and pink-flowered thrift ran riot over the walls of his village. In the company of his dog, he wandered among the rocks below his house to see what might be found. After a while he heard a faint cry, then another, so weak that it was barely audible above the rumble of the waves.

He followed the sound, which led him across a clutter of boulders that ringed a small depression in the shore. At high tide, the surf surged freely in and out, but when the water was at low ebb, the place became a tidal pool, isolated from the great mother sea by a stretch of sand and green-mottled rocks. Was it land then, or was it sea? It was neither, and both: an in-between place, its boundaries shifting with every mood of the moon. At such mutable, magical spots, strange spirits might enter the mortal world, as one had done on this day. Lutey peered down into the circle of rocks. His gaze was met by sea green eyes from another age and realm.

They were frightened eyes, set in a sweet, pale face half-hidden by red-gold hair. This being was clearly female from head to waist, but at the hips, her body faded into a long, smooth shape, a shimmering iridescence beneath the surface of the pool. Lutey stood gaping, still as a tree. He had found a mermaid.

"Help me," she whimpered. "Help me to the water." She thrashed in the shallow pool. Lutey advanced cautiously down the rocks, wading through a flurry of tiny fish and crabs to her side.

"I can give you powers, if only you will get me to the sea," she said, raising her arms with the gesture of a trustful child.

Lutey bent and lifted her from the water. The sea-maiden was as light as a cloud. She wrapped her arms around his neck as he bore her up over the lip of rock that rimmed the pool and picked his way down to the furrowed stretch of sand. From among the rocks behind him trotted his dog, whining nervously.

At the water's edge, he halted. The mermaid looked up into his face and made a nestling movement in his arms. "Tell me your heart's desire," she murmured. "And you shall have it, whatever it may be."

Lutey looked out to sea for a moment. Then he said, "I want the power to break evil spells." Witchcraft was an age-old practice in his remote, sea-ringed land. A disgruntled Cornish villager could bring misfortune on a neighbor merely by ill-wishing; the man who could reverse such spells would be sought after indeed.

The sea-maiden smiled and ran a delicate finger along his face. "It is done," she said. "And what other boon?"

Lutey was in the water now, breakers foaming about his knees. "I want the magic to cast healing spells."

"Done," she said. "And another?"

"I want these powers for my sons and for their sons and for their sons' sons after that, so that my family's name will be honored for all time."

"You have it," said the mermaid. "For your kindness, you shall have all these gifts." As a pledge, she drew from her hair the ivory comb that held it, and the long tresses cascaded about her shoulders and creamy breast. She pressed the comb into his hand. Standing in the sea, Lutey felt the dizzying pull of the tide. His feet sank deeper into the sand with every wave that broke about him, and at the shore's edge, his dog set up a howl. The mermaid laughed, tightening her hold on his neck. Droplets of water sparkled on her lashes. Now the two of them were in her element. She pulled his head down so that her mouth was at his ear. "Stay with me," she whispered. "What pleasures have you left on the shore?"

Lutey choked and struggled; the frail arms were surprisingly strong, and his feet slipped on the sea floor. The dog was pulling at his trouser leg. Stumbling in the shallow surf, he let go of the mermaid. Instinctively, he drew out his pocket knife. At the sight of it, the sea-maiden gave a powerful kick of her tail, arching out of reach. Like many creatures of the other world, she was repelled by iron.

"Farewell," she sang then. "For nine years I will bide. Then we shall meet again." She gave a leap that took her into deep water, and the last Lutey saw of her was the streaming, flamelike hair, vanishing into the green sea. Urged by his dog, he struggled to the shore and climbed to the cottage, with the comb clutched in one hand and the knife in the other.

His wife stood watching him from the door. "What's this, now?" she said. "Wet to the skin, and naught but a bit of bone to show for an afternoon's wrecking?"

"It's a comb," Lutey said sullenly.

"A comb, is it!" replied his wife. "It's a row of teeth on a shark jaw."

Lutey looked at it and discovered that this was true. "Yet I'll keep it," he said, and walked past her into the cottage. He carefully hung his prize on a beam, amid the clutter of fish nets and wooden buoys and drying frames suspended there. Then he spread his wet clothes before the fire to dry, and ate in silence the food his wife set before him. After supper the woman turned her stolid profile to him and bent to her sewing. Lutey went early to bed, staring up at the sea-maiden's strange token until the sea outside sent him to sleep with its ceaseless song.

It was on a day soon after, as Lutey walked the high road near his village, that the mermaid's promise was first fulfilled. In a wind-stunted tangle of hawthorn trees, he saw a farmer kneeling beside a dead cow. This was but one of many, the man said, tight-lipped. His herd was cursed, but who had done it he did not know.

Che fisherman knelt down. "A witch has done this," he said. "Bleed the next cow that falls ill, and catch the blood on a pile of straw. When it dries, set fire to the straw, and mark well the first person who passes through the smoke. That is your ill-wisher. Then deal with the witch how you will." He was silent for a moment, listening with surprise to his own words.

"Aye," the farmer said, with no further comment.

The odd prescription brought swift results. Word of Lutey's cleverness passed quickly about the village of Cury.

It was a child Lutey saved next: A man came asking for him late one night, and with lantern in hand led him to a poor, cramped cottage down the bay. The mother looked up from the pallet where her young one lay, racked with fever.

"The tide's turning is close at hand," she said anxiously. The belief was strong that death came only on the ebbing tide; if the sick one could be held fast through the turning until the flood tide set in, there would be another six hours of grace.

Lutey carried the child outside, down a rocky path to a grove where a sapling stood in the shadow of its great parent tree. It was an ash, the tree Englishmen held sacred, for reasons long forgotten. Into its branches Lutey gently thrust the child. And at the moment that marked the slack between the ebb and flood of the sea, the magic of the ages touched the saplings. The child's fever broke.

By autumn, when the pilchard were running, Lutey had no time left for fishing. His reputation as a peller—so named because he could expel spirits of sickness and evil—had spread far beyond Cury and Lizard Point. The poor folk came to Lutey in times of trouble, bearing jugs of fish oil or lengths of stout rope for payment if they could afford no more. It seemed there was nothing he did not know. He kept a bit of hangman's rope for the curing of scrofula,

Beautiful and terrible were the creatures of the sea, as a Cornishman found when he saved a mermaid. She rewarded him with magic powers for a while; then she took him from his people, to dwell forever in the depths.

and sold written charms to wear around the neck for warding off ill wishes. He knew the secret recipes for medicines made from charred mice and scabious root—the devil's-bit so prized for its healing powers. One by one, the sons of Lutey tied up their boats and joined him. They, too, understood the power of angelica leaves and elder blossom to cure a cold, and groundsel to stop the fevered shivers of ague. The art of healing came to them in the same mysterious way, as if through the water they bathed in and the air they breathed. Lutey kept to himself the source of the gift, and the comb he held in covenant through winters of endless misty rain and summers bright with yellow gorse.

After a few years, he moved to a larger dwelling in the village, a house that boasted an upper story and many rooms to please his fretful wife. But he grew more withdrawn with the years and often returned to the old stone cottage at low tide to sit alone by the tidal pool.

One day, abruptly, he took his herring nets and headed toward the sea. "Going to fish," was all he said.

But it was no day for fishing. In the harbor of the village, angry waves slapped at the boats. Along the shore, the sky was thick with clouds that scudded before a threatening wind. Lutey's sons exchanged glances, and the youngest followed the old man to see that no harm would befall him. In the end, though, the son was helpless against the force that moved his father. Lutey had pushed a small skiff into the water; it bobbed and pitched in the chop, but he made no move to guide it. Pale arms and a bright head flashed around and around the little vessel. The mermaid was sporting in the waves, still young and fair, although the mortal man's hair was thin and streaked with gray. While the son watched from shore, the sea-maiden beckoned. Lutey rose to his feet, lurching in the swells. "My hour is come," he shouted at his son. Then the father plunged into the water and was gone. Later, the youth would report that the sea seemed simply to have swallowed Lutey alive. And in a sense it did: For with that plunge, the old man had crossed a boundary into another world, a world as old and fathomless as time itself. The mermaid had him now, drawing him down and down through corridors of hazy green to her sea cave nestled far below the Cornish shore. Whether he ever regretted leaving the life of men and boats, whether the mermaid's dwelling was humble or fine, whether she kept to him only or had others as well, no one ever knew. Lutey was never seen on earth above again. The mermaid's magic endured through his kin (for generations, the Luteys of Cury were renowned for their powers against sickness and witchcraft), but she took her payment all the same. It was said that every nine years, as regularly as the tides, one of his descendants was lost at sea.

Such tales of magic once were common among peoples who clung to the fringes of the

land, for their lives were dominated by the sea. How deep was it, and how far beyond the visible horizon did it extend? It was older than anything else humankind knew, ever-changing, yet always the same: Nations rose and flourished and passed away, but the waters that bathed their shores endured through the generations.

In the pageant of mortal lives, the sea played many roles. It was both cradle and grave, the wellspring of life and its destroyer. It was both alien and kindred, a link connecting the finite shore to the mysterious realm of the infinite. It lured men from the land: Even the earliest farming tribes had members struck by sea fever—sailors who fashioned makeshift vessels and rode upon the sea's broad, heaving back to find adventure. They took great risks. All seafarers faced, of course, the hazards of tempest, rock and reef. A few told of threats more terrifying still, spirit-demons that haunted the deep to torment and feed upon human intruders. Some, it was said, were monstrous creatures who had survived in the ocean depths since the birth of the world. Others were ghosts of men and ships that had perished at sea, and now, it seemed, were returning to lure the living to the same fate.

Sinister spirits dwelled, too, in freshwater lakes and streams, and in pools that welled up far inland from the coast, from invisible sources deep within the earth. These watery creatures could assume various forms, both foul and fair. Many seemed perfectly human, and were as sweetly seductive as the mermaid who lured the Cornishman Lutey right off the face of the earth. All were sons and daughters of the primal waters that had once enveloped the universe, and at the core of their being was a powerful pagan magic inimical to emergent civilizations.

To the ancients, this magic had no bounds; under the pretext of worship, they sought to steal it away for their own use. Stories were told of certain rare waters that could bestow wisdom on mortals and gods, could cure disease and cleanse the soul of evil, could restore youth to the aged or even bring the dead to life.

The Hindus of India held sacred the Ganges, for example, and traveled great distances to purify themselves in its wide, muddy shallows as it flowed southeast from the Himalayas, across the subcontinent and into the Bay of Bengal. The devout carried small vials of the murky water to use as a charm against evil spirits, to place in the mouth of a dying person, or to sprinkle over bridal couples as a symbol of fertility. The river was created, it was said, as an earthly embodiment of the Hindu goddess Gangā, who was ordered down from heaven to bless and sanctify the young race of humans. But Gangā came so hard and angry to this watery fall that the compassionate god Śiva intervened, to shield the fragile earth from the impact of her landing. Śiva caught heaven's torrent on his mighty brow and channeled its flow through the labyrinth of his tangled hair.

Other magic waters bubbled up from clefts in the earth's crust—hot springs and mineral fountains that seemed meant for healing and rejuvenation. With blinded eyes and wasted limbs, generations of the faithful trudged to these pools, hoping to bathe away their afflictions. The Celts told of a pool of miraculous water – the Well of the World – that had the power to restore life to dead men and could revive those turned to stone by enchantment.

Wisdom was believed to reside in the water emanating at some points on the earth's surface. It was said that Odin, the supreme Norse god, in his relentless quest for knowledge, sacrificed one of his eyes for the privilege of drinking from such a rare well. The spring was hidden deep within the twisted roots of the cosmic tree from which the world had been formed, and was infused with a magic so potent that a single draught of the cool, bubbling waters brought a flood of insight and understanding, accompanied by an undying thirst for more wisdom still.

And everywhere in the impoverished, disease-ridden world of earlier days, people thirsted for the waters of youth – the secret fountains where fairies supposedly dipped their children to free them from the time-bound flesh of mortality. For men and women who could expect to grow old before they had seen forty summers pass, the notion must have been irresistible: to recover from cool water the youth that had so quickly flown; to wade in with wrinkled, weathered skin and emerge with flesh made smooth and lovely again. Rumors of the *vijarâ nadâ* – or "ageless river" – flowed through the songs of India, and the Japanese spoke of a fountain of youth hidden on the summit of the sacred Mount Fuji.

Most of the tales of waters of youth were simply legends, so twisted and colored in their passage through the ages that they lost any connection they may have had to real events. Ultimately, the truest and greatest miracle wrought by water was the creation of life itself. In humans, it coursed through the veins as the primordial component of blood; it flowed from the breast as milk to nurture the infant that had journeyed into earthly existence floating in the private sea of its mother's womb. In the world around, rain brought the wonder of nourishing grasses, rising straight and green; primitive men spied a band of trees snaking across a parched plain and knew that a life-giving stream could be found there. The earliest settlements gathered around rivers and springs and natural harbors: Jericho, perhaps the oldest known city on earth, grew around a never-failing water source in a desert.

To early peoples, life's original awakening seemed inevitably linked to water. Year after year they watched the Nile rise to cover the earth; then, as the flood slowly subsided, the familiar points of land began to reappear. It must have been thus, they reasoned, at the very dawn of time – the contours of the earth taking shape gradually from a primeval waste of waters. Many ancient races shared this idea, imagining that the cosmos was formed from an expanse of waters without bounds or direction – no east or west, no up or down, only darkness and the infinite deep.

Each culture imagined differently, however, how the world emerged from this great ocean. To the Egyptians, the infant earth began as a hollow bubble floating in the watery firmament. An Indian myth tells how a great tree rose from the deep, and how in time a worm was born in the tree. The worm began to eat of the wood, and age upon age, as sawdust fell into the water, the world slowly was formed.

Two thousand miles westward, in the fertile region between the Tigris and Euphrates Rivers, the Babylonians described the mingling of salt water and sweet water—the mother-creature Tiamat and the father Apsu—to create the first race of gods. Their offspring, it was said, shaped the heavens and earth from the primal sea.

And far to the north, in Finland, the ancients portrayed creation as the work of Ilmatar, the lonely Virgin Mother of the Water. Impregnated by the rough caresses of the wind and waves, she took a broken sea bird's egg and from it made a world to house her unborn child. One fragment of shattered shell she set as the arching dome of the heavens above, and another as the unformed lump of earth below. The egg's yolk and white became the sun and moon, and the mottled specks turned into stars.

Still heavy with child, Ilmatar then shaped the world: Her hands formed sea bed and headlands, and her feet hollowed out ocean caves. Islands and continents she sang into being, smoothing the coastlines with her side. When she finished, she bore the first man, Vainamöinen. Grown to impatient manhood in Ilmatar's womb, he clawed his way through bone and flesh until he swam free. In time he waded onto a nameless shore to admire the world his mother had made and to sow the seeds that would bear fruits and grains and flowers.

But the stolid earth and its inhabitants were no match for the parent sea. Water was a fickle force, full of shifting moods and contradiction: The rivers that watered the land could be turned into juggernauts by snowmelt in the mountains where they rose. Earthquakes deep below the fish-crowded seas could send crushing tidal waves against unsuspecting shores half a world away, obliterating entire cities.

It seems, however, that at one point in history a flood more cataclysmic than any known before or since occurred. What its causes were, no one could say for sure. Chroniclers of the terror suggested that the gods were angered at mortals and so sent the deluge to destroy the human race.

This story of punishment by flood, with variations, was told in many lands and struck fear in every heart. The Roman poet Ovid recounted the story well. The world-devastating flood he described was inflicted on the early Greeks by Zeus, god of thunder. When the deluge began, lightning flashed and thunder cracked. A screaming wind hurled torrents of rain upon the world, and the very earth split open to unleash subterranean streams.

The ordered world, the poet said, became a terrifying chaos. One might see a peasant thrashing past the roof of what was once his cottage, striving toward high ground, while another rowed his skiff over a field he had plowed only yesterday. "Someone catches fish in the top of a tree, or an anchor drags in meadowland, or the keel brushes grape arbors under water," wrote Ovid. "The wolf swims with the lamb . . . wandering birds look long, in vain, for landing places, and tumble, ex-

From water, goodness sprang. Somewhere in the world, it was said, there
bubbled a spring that restored youth to the aged and vigor to the frail. On its
surface, old men and women saw themselves again as they once had been.

Water could bring death as well as life, as mortals knew too well. In the time
before history, divine wrath unleashed a raging flood that drowned the entire world.

The maritime mirror-world

According to some sages, the formation of the world was wrought with such perfect symmetry that every creature living on land had a counterpart in the sea. The mirror images of mortal men and women were mermen and mermaids, who ruled underwater kingdoms. And these kingdoms teemed with a wonderful menagerie. The Swedish naturalist Olaus Magnus described fish-tailed horses that ranged the ocean from Brittany to Norway; he also spoke of dogfish that attacked and devoured human swimmers. And the Roman historian Aelian reported that the seas surrounding the Island of Taprobana – later called Ceylon – provided watery pastures for ram-headed fish and forests for scaly, swimming lions, sea elephants and other exotic marine mammals.

hausted, into the sea. The deep's great license has buried all the hills, and new waves thunder against the mountaintops. The flood has taken all things, or nearly all, and those whom water, by chance, has spared, starvation slowly conquers."

By most accounts, at least one virtuous human couple was forewarned of the deluge and allowed to survive it, so that the cleansed earth might be repopulated after the floodwaters subsided. In this way the terrible end became a new beginning.

Zeus himself chose two to survive the flood described by Ovid – an old man named Deucalion and his good wife, Pyrrha, who rowed to safety on the peak of Mount Parnassus. At first, nothing but the topmost mountain peaks protruded above the floodwaters, so that the survivors found themselves enshrouded by clouds. For nine days and as many nights, the couple lamented the world that lay drowned beneath them. Then, gradually, the waters ebbed and gave the world back again. The sea regained its shores, and the rivers their channels. Deucalion and his wife wept at the desolate landscape that met their eyes, a wilderness dotted with mud-coated trees, and nowhere a sign of human life.

Too old for childbearing, the couple did as the god instructed. They picked up stones from the sodden earth and, one by one, flung the stones behind them. Then the stones softened and took human shape, resembling half-finished statues. In time they turned to flesh and blood – those thrown by Pyrrha becoming women and those by Deucalion, men. This tale explains, perhaps, why the Greeks are called *laoi*, from the word for "stone."

The Water Horse

Of the great flood's survivors, the most widely known is, of course, the Hebrew patriarch Noah. But his story is not the oldest. The Biblical account echoes a far more ancient tale that drifted westward from Mesopotamia, the fertile, flood-ridden region where the Tigris and Euphrates met. Here, chroniclers told old tales of an elder named Ut-napishtim, who was warned in a dream of an impending flood sent by the gods of the Sumerian civilization to punish unruly mortals. The message came to Ut-napishtim deep in the night, as if whispered through the reed walls of his hut by a sympathetic deity: He must tear down his house and build a boat.

In the morning, on a field beside the Euphrates, Ut-napishtim laid the keel and ribs of a vessel whose length and width formed a square 120 cubits—about 180 feet—on a side. This ship had six decks in all, and the top deck was roofed to keep out the rains. The planking was sealed with asphalt-like bitumen, which was abundant in the surrounding marshland. When Ut-napishtim was finished, he gathered together under the ark's vaulted roof his kinsfolk. He also brought along craftsmen to carry human skills into the new world—masons and scribes, potters and smiths, weavers and tanners, sailors and merchants, those who tilled the land and fished the sea. And he took into the boat a male and female of all the beasts of the earth—not only sheep and cattle, but the

The Sea Dog

snake and lion and scorpion as well, so that no species would be lost.

The storm sent by the gods began in the night, as if to catch people unaware. For six days and nights it raged, while Ut-napishtim and his company huddled in the lurching ark. When the clouds broke on the seventh morning, Ut-napishtim opened his wooden hatches to let the sun stream in. For many more days, the vessel drifted in a flat, endless waste of water. It grounded at last, tilted at a crazy angle, in a shallow niche on a mountainside. But no land appeared where the voyagers could alight; water lapped gently at the vessel's sides. The old man gently drew a dove from its cage and let the bird fly free above

The Lion of the Deep

the sea's surface. But the dove found no resting place, and so it returned. The next day's test revealed the same: A tiny swallow freed by Ut-napishtim returned to the boat, exhausted. On the third day, he let go a raven. This bird did not return. It had found a spot to land, signifying that the killing waters were withdrawing.

As the waters receded, the human passengers crawled down from the boat onto the muddy ground. The craftsmen and their wives set about the work of rebuilding the world the flood had wiped away. Ut-napishtim and his wife were not to live in this world, however. For their faithful obedience to the whispered will of the gods, they were rewarded with something much dearer than glory or power. They received the gift of immortality and were carried away beyond the temporal world

to a paradise at the mouth of the great rivers, an ageless island set like a gleaming green jewel in the sea of the rising sun. Here, in solitary peace, they were set to be guardians over the mystery of life.

In the ages that followed, one man — a descendant of the flood's survivors — went seeking Ut-napishtim there. This man was the Sumerian warrior-king Gilgamesh, famed in the world that sprang up in the wake of the great flood. On the rich plain between the Tigris and Euphrates, Gilgamesh raised the city of Erech, a strong-walled citadel of whitewashed houses and flowering gardens. Indeed, pleasures flowered there in every quarter. At the city's center towered a ziggurat, a many-tiered temple that formed a stairway to heaven. In the winding streets below, the bazaar's close-packed stalls were pungent with the smell of spices, and noisy with the bleating of sheep and the shouts of merchants.

The dwelling of Gilgamesh was a wide and airy palace with bright-hued mosaics inlaid on every wall. But there came a day when all of Erech's pleasures seemed as nothing. Death struck down the great King's lifelong companion, the friend of his childhood and youth. Day after day, Gilgamesh knelt beside a brick-lined grave in the shadow of the city wall. Within lay a body bedecked with earrings and armlets of gold, flanked by the drinking cup and spear of the warrior. Flies buzzed around the treasure; the beloved flesh reeked in the heat as it decayed. The King had done all that could be done, but his companion was bound for the world of the dead—a realm of smothering dust and darkness beneath the flat disk of the earth, where mortals sat languishing in misery for all eternity. No one had hope of escaping this fate.

For seven days and nights without ceasing Gilgamesh wept. On the eighth day he rose and walked away from the city walls. He put behind him the orchards and gardens and the tidy fields laced with irrigation canals. He had only one thought—to find Ut-napishtim, survivor of the ancient flood, and learn the secret of immortality that the elder was said to guard.

Soon the warrior-king lost count of the days. With an animal's blind hunger, he killed the beasts that crossed his path—the ibex and panther, hyena and lion. From those he could not eat he took skins to clothe his limbs, and coverings to warm him when he slept at night under the star-fretted heavens. Near the sluggish mouths of the rivers, where the flats gave way to marshland, he poled slowly across the desolate expanse of shallows in a slim canoe. The silence was broken only by the cries of the ducks and herons nesting in the reeds.

At length a mountain rose up before him, blocking his path. It was a place Gil-

The Oceanic Elephant

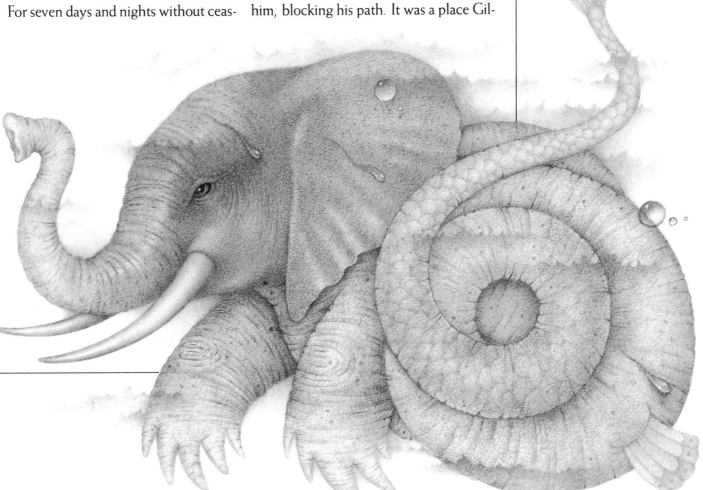

gamesh had heard tales of, but had never seen – the boundary of the mortal world. The mountain's twin peaks, stretching up to pierce the clouds, stood guard over the rising and setting of the sun. Its roots descended deep into the realm of the dead. There was no way around; the passage to the other side lay through the heart of darkness, a tunnel filled with the gloom of the grave. Beyond it lay the unknown world where Ut-napishtim dwelled.

Unflinching, the warrior-king marched into a mouth that yawned in the mountainside. He stumbled through blackness so complete that he could see nothing before him and nothing behind. It pressed on him from all sides, cold and damp, and seemed to squeeze the air from his breast. His groping hands touched walls that oozed with slime and crawled with small scurrying things. Gilgamesh flicked them from his skin and blindly pushed on, for hours and then days. Finally, a pinpoint of light appeared far ahead. A little later, he stumbled into the warm breath of day – blinded now not by darkness, but by the light of the sun. Then the contours of another world took shape around him.

He was in a garden where no mortal had ever walked before. The flowers were of pearls and sky blue lapis lazuli. They had leaves of jade and tiny spikes of agate where thorns would have been. Overhead, silver grapevines sagged under clusters of blood red carnelian. Gilgamesh descended through this glittering forest to the shores of a broad, dark sea. In the distance, a green island was faintly visible in the mist that curled from the restless waters, thick with poison and fraught with danger. This was the retreat of Ut-napishtim, ageless, deathless guardian of the secret of mortality. And near to Gilgamesh a young woman sat, making wine in a golden bowl.

She looked at the man before her – a travel-worn pilgrim in tattered skins, with sunken cheeks and matted beard. Even in that place, though, his name was known.

"Gilgamesh," she said. "Why do you come wandering here?"

When she heard of his grief and his challenge to death, she reproached him with a laugh. "You will never find what you are seeking," she said. "Better to wash the dust of the road from your hair, and be glad of the life within your grasp. Enjoy the clasp of a little child's hand, and the warmth of a woman's arms. To live forever is not the lot of man."

But Gilgamesh would not be halted, and at length, the guardian of the shore agreed to help. She led him to Ut-napishtim's ferryman, who plied the deadly waters of mortality in the service of the immortal.

With eyes that glowered under shaggy brows, the boatman examined the wayfarer, then threw another obstacle in his path. It was impossible just now to make the crossing, the boatman said, gesturing toward his barque, a sad little reed-built vessel with a carved serpent prow. The boat's mast was missing, and its oarlocks were in disrepair; there would be no way across except by poling, and he had no poles.

Gilgamesh set his jaw, and stalked into the forest. He had endured too much to be thwarted by a reed boat now. The warrior drew his ax and cut poles for the crossing.

Then the two men set forth across the waters of death. Gilgamesh himself poled the barque, being careful not to let the poisonous currents that boiled about the little craft splash upon his skin. Because the poles were envenomed by the water, he released each one into the sea as he used it. When the poles were gone, Gilgamesh, ever-resourceful, stood and made his tall body serve as a mast. His arms he held out for spars, and his garments he stretched out for a sail. In this way he brought himself to the island of eternal life.

Ut-napishtim waited on the shore to greet the King of Erech. The ancient one was strong and brown from his centuries in the sun, and indeed he looked no older than the travel-weary mortal. Gilgamesh sat with the old man on that radiant island, where grief and pain were strangers and death had no power, and again he told the reasons for his journey. When he was finished, Ut-napishtim only shook his head, as the others had done.

"There is no permanence in the world," the old man said. "Is a house built to stand forever? Does the river's floodtime endure? Birth and death are bound together in men's destiny."

But Gilgamesh would not be swayed.

"How is it that you alone have won the secret of life?" he inquired, seeking an excuse to linger. Then Ut-napishtim described the great flood and its aftermath, the events of ages past that had brought him there. On the sand of the shore, he sketched the outline of the massive ark he had built, and told how he had divided it into nine sections with sturdy bulkheads in-between, so that each species might have a private chamber in which to ride out the storm. He detailed the terrors of the deluge, of the fearful nether waters unleashed from deep within the earth, of storm clouds lit by hellish lightning and rains that slashed across the ship's deck in blinding sheets.

And he told of the gods' remorse when it was over and their promise to the new earth's pioneers: Humanity might be punished, in its reborn age, by the ravages of lion and wolf, by pestilence and famine and war. But never again would tempest and flood annihilate the entire race.

When the old man's tale was done, Gilgamesh still wanted what he had come for.

"The life you are seeking is not mine to give, nor man's to hold," Ut-napishtim said wearily. "If you would taste of immortality, put yourself to this test: Resist sleep for six days and seven nights."

Gilgamesh sank into slumber even before Ut-napishtim's words were finished. Six days on end he slept.

To drive home the lesson, Ut-napishtim told his wife to bake a loaf of bread each day and place it by the mortal's head. On the seventh day, Gilgamesh awoke and stretched. He rose to his feet. Then the ancient one showed him his weakness—and the indomitable powers of time—in the humble loaves of bread. The loaf baked on the first day was already hard as a stone. The loaf from the second day was like leather. The third loaf was sodden with spoilage, and the fourth crusted with mold. The fifth showed the first signs of mildew, and the sixth was

In search of the secret of immortality, the Sumerian warrior-king Gilgamesh journeyed through dark caverns to the edge of a sea. Offshore shimmered an island—the home of a sage who knew how to elude death's clutches.

A pool lay deep in the ocean floor—an enchanted water within water. Here grew a flower that preserved human life, and Gilgamesh dived to pluck it.

fresh. As for the seventh, it was still warm from the oven. But Gilgamesh grasped the message. He had no appetite for bread.

"You must return home now," Ut-napishtim said kindly, and to the ferryman he said, "Go. You who brought the mortal here are banished into the mortal's world. Follow him." At the moment of departure, however, Ut-napishtim's wife saw hope still burning in the mortal's eyes. She spoke a word to her husband, and Ut-napishtim nodded gravely.

"If you would taste of immortality still, Gilgamesh, then I will reveal to you a certain secret of the sea." And then the old man told him of an herb that flowered in a magic offshore pool, guarded closely by those waters since the dawn of time. The plant was hidden deep, and protective thorns lined its stalk. But the one who was strong and brave enough to pluck the plant had only to taste of it to absorb its timeless magic. It had the power to restore youth, and so eternally to renew life.

Gilgamesh leaped to his feet. With the banished boatman, he set the reed barque upon a flowing stream. Its waters carried them past the roiling waters of death, into the deepest channel of the ocean and straight to the place where the sea pool lay. Gilgamesh plunged into the waters and swam deep, deeper than any mortal had descended before. He found there, just as Ut-napishtim had foretold, the sheltered grotto where the pink flower grew. Its fragile petals and shadowy green leaves waved, as if beckoning to his outstretched hand. He grasped; thorns tore at his hands until his blood streamed out in crimson rivulets. Some-

unfortunate voyagers looked their last on life, and clutched the gold that would aid their ghosts in the watery underworld.

The people of Norse coasts knew when the sea-goddess had embraced their kin. On winter nights, the wraiths of those

who had drowned would trail across the beaches to the little settlements and drink the ale from the midwinter feasts.

To appease the voracious hunger of the sea, Norsemen made sacrificial offerings. Of the captives from their raids,

one man in ten was sent into the deep to feed the goddess Ran and, it was hoped, ensure safe passage for the rest.

Chapter Two

Daring the Sea-gods' Realm

The oldest of all sea quests began thirty centuries ago, when the elder gods still ruled the world and had not yet retreated before the advancing tide of humankind. The adventurer was Jason, Prince of Iolcus on the northeast coast of Greece, who had spent his youth hidden in the groves of Mount Pelion, receiving tutelage from the Centaur Chiron. Jason had been sent into Chiron's care because his murderous uncle Pelias had usurped his father's throne and his parents feared for the boy's life. When he reached manhood, however, Jason came down from Chiron's mountain alone and challenged his uncle, demanding his rightful inheritance. This happened on the feast day of Poseidon, lord of horses, Earthshaker, god of the sea. Pelias, who claimed Poseidon for his father, could not desecrate the rites by murdering his nephew, but he was not inclined to give up the throne. He regarded Jason narrowly for some moments. Then he stat-

ed his terms for the surrender of Iolcus.

"Bring to me the golden ram's fleece that hangs in the oak wood of the King of Colchis," he said. "Journey there by sea."

This was naming the impossible. Such a voyage would take Jason across the Aegean, where capricious gods and spirits ruled, and from there into unknown territories commanded by beings no one cared even to describe. Colchis itself was remote: It lay on the shores of the Black Sea, whose entrance was guarded by a magic that no mortal had ever defeated. And the Colchian King was unlikely to relinquish so venerable a treasure as a fleece of gold.

It was for just such quests as this, however, that Jason had been bred and schooled. The Centaur Chiron, half horse, half man, was a tutor of heroes: Hercules of Tiryns and Achilles and the master physician Asclepius had all spent their childhoods in the dark and whispering pine forests of Chiron's mountain, learning from him the arts of healing and of music and of warfare. Jason agreed to the venture and acted at once: He sent heralds throughout Greece, calling for companions. He was eagerly answered.

The following year, on an April morning when waves slapped smartly against the stone mole that formed the harbor of Iolcus, the company of Jason assembled for the voyage. At the water's edge, leaning on tall leather shields, their oiled skin gleaming and their eyes narrowed in the bright light, were fifty of the finest warriors of Greece.

Among them were Hercules of Tiryns, the strongest of men; wily Theseus of Athens, who in Crete had slain the Minotaur; Orpheus of Thrace, who could charm the very beasts of the field with the music of his lyre; Tiphys of Boeotian Siphae, the most skilled of helmsmen; Nauplius and Euphemus of Taenarus, sons of Poseidon; the Spartan warrior twins Castor and Polydeuces; keen-eyed Lynceus, who could see things hidden below the earth; Mopsus the Lapith, skilled in augury; and Acastus of Iolcus, Pelias' own son, who, against his father's wishes, had insisted on the venture. One woman was there: Atalanta of Calydon, fierce and long-legged, a famed runner and huntress. And the builder of Jason's ship was there: Argus of Thespiae. His name meant "swift," and it had been given to the ship he had built.

The ship itself lay now on log rollers that had been placed in a trough hollowed out from the shingle at the water's edge. She was a long and slender galley, undecked and open to the elements. Into her curving bowsprit was built the branch of a tree, the oak of Dodona, which grew above a shrine sacred to Athena, goddess of wisdom. Some said, in fact, that Athena herself had fashioned the prow for Argus and that the wood had the power to speak and tell men of their destiny. At the bow were painted two eyes, which kept a perpetual vigil against magic.

On this day of departure, there were rituals to be observed. Beside the water, Jason and his men raised an altar to Apollo, god of embarkation. Two oxen were slaughtered and their thigh bones wrapped in rolls of fat. The men kindled a fire of olive logs on the altar and thrust the offerings into it. And onto the flames, as was seemly, they poured a libation of wine and water, which made the flames flare high, sending the smoke of supplication into the heavens.

After that came the launching. The men wedged oars against the leather tholepins that lined the *Argo's* bulwarks and heaved themselves forward. Groaning and smoking from the friction, the *Argo* slid down the rollers into the harbor. She rocked gently in the shallow water, alive to wind and wave. From her bow issued a cry of summoning, as if the ship was eager to fare forward. The men said the cry came from the sacred oak itself.

Within moments, the company had settled in pairs on the rowing benches, stowing their weapons underneath. They watched, oars held upright in salute, as Jason, the captain, made a final offering to the gods who ruled the seas: He poured an offering of honey and wine into the water all around the *Argo*. Sailors knew well that

The Greek heroes who sailed with Jason in the Argo counted on magic and divine aid to avert the perils of the sea. The ship bore painted eyes upon her bow to spy out enemies; at her prow reared an oak branch that held the spirit of the goddess Athena.

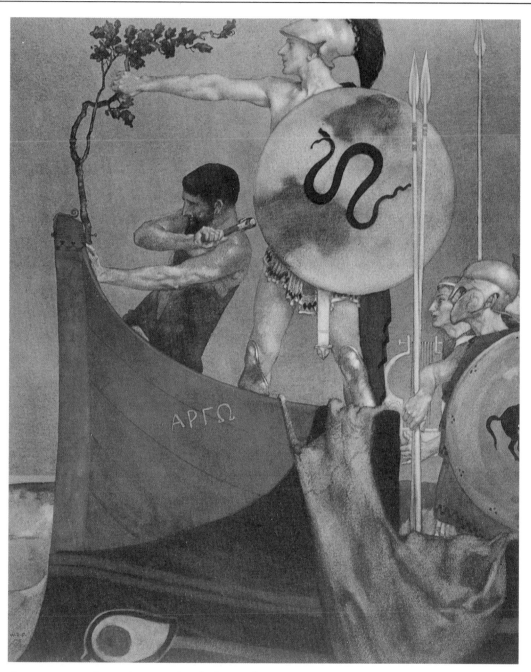

they trespassed in a domain that belonged to powerful and ancient deities, and they always paid the proper homage.

When the wine was poured out, fifty oars sliced into the water as one, and the *Argo* surged toward the morning sun. A wake of foam spread out behind her. From the rocky shore, the Centaur Chiron called his blessing after the seafarers and watched them until the *Argo* was no more than a speck in the waters of the Pagasaean Gulf. As the sun rose high, they rounded a headland and sped onto the lapis blue waters of the open Aegean.

Pine-covered Skiathos fell to port. At their backs the wind picked up, and they shipped oars and stepped the mast, lifting the heavy timber from its resting place in the hull and setting it firmly into a crossplank amidships. They made the timber fast with stays drawn fore and aft; they unfurled the broad linen sail from the yardarm. The sail bellied and strained at the sheets.

Now the men rested on their benches. In the stern, his hand firm on the long steering oar, the helmsman Tiphys stood guiding the *Argo* as she ran before the breeze. If wise eyes watched the sailors from the foam or from the sea's depths, there was no sign.

They headed northeast across the Aegean, making for the Phrygian coast. There, they would have to negotiate the narrow passage of the Hellespont and sail across the Sea of Propontis. Then, if they could navigate the Bosporus and gain the inland sea, they had only to crawl along the north coast of Asia Minor to reach Colchis on its distant shore.

The journey's beginning was marked by fair days and mild, when the wind blew steadily at the seafarers' backs, allowing them to rest and dream along the sun-sparked sea road. The broad expanse of the Aegean was strewn with mountain islands. One after another, they appeared. First no more than a dark smudge on the horizon, each took on vivid lines and hues as it drew near. Shimmering gray olive orchards appeared, set against the green of young crops. On rocky hillsides, sheep could be seen grazing. Then the details drifted back into blue haze, and another island rose above the horizon to beguile the eyes.

Some days, however, the sailors had hard work; the ship's sail could be used only if the wind was abaft the beam. When the breeze shifted forward, the Argonauts unstepped the wooden mast, stowed it with its sail furled inside the *Argo's* hull and bent to their oars. Orpheus took his stance in the bow, then, and paced their strokes with his lyre.

Whether by sail or oar, the Argonauts hugged coastlines where they could, or made short hops from island to island. They sailed by day and steered toward land each evening, scanning the shore for dark slashes that signaled the mouths of rivers. In the shelter of such backwaters, out of view of pirates and marauders, the men could beach the craft. Then they would hunt and fill their water jars and finally settle by the *Argo* to sleep out the night under the wheeling stars.

But landings such as these were only the kindest of the Argonauts' adventures. Their way was marked by perils. They had to slip through the Hellespont at night to avoid the soldiers of the King of Troy, who guarded the strait. On the island of Arctonnessus in the Sea of Propontis, they battled six-armed earth-giants. Later, driven ashore by a gale, they were attacked by a troop of warriors, whom they slaughtered. In the morning, however, they discovered that the warriors served a petty king who had given the Argonauts shelter only a few nights earlier and so was a hearth friend. They were stained with blood guilt, and they felt the wrath of the gods of the place: Storm clouds gathered around them, and the sea wind howled for twelve days, whipping the waves into mountains and lashing the shore with icy rain. The weather cleared only after they sacrificed to Rhea, mother of the earth that the slaying had polluted.

Farther along the coast, Hercules' beloved companion Hylas was seduced out of the world by a water nymph; distraught, Hercules left the company. At Salmydessus, in eastern Thrace, the Argonauts delivered a king from the torture of Harpies – foul, winged women who had laid waste his land. In return, the old man told them how to meet the central terror of the journey – the guardians of the Bosporus, the strait that gave passage to the inland sea.

So the Argonauts took to sea again, rowing now through endless rain and wind, fighting their way against the powerful currents of the Bosporus to reach the place where monsters waited. They heard the noise of their foes long in advance of any sighting. It sounded like the rhythmic rolling of far-off thunder, but it grew into a series of deafening roars. Then, in a winding passage walled by rocky crags, they saw the enemy, wreathed in mist and sea spume.

This was the Symplegades, or "clashing rocks." Mindless, speechless, ancient creatures of the sea, the Symplegades were two black pinnacles floating free in the waves. As the men backed water, the crags – no more than ten boat lengths ahead – rocked slowly apart, then clapped together with a cry of rage and hunger that resounded against the Bosporus' cliffs. Spray flew toward the *Argo*, drenching the seafarers huddled over their oars. The rocks snapped asunder again, forming currents that sucked at the ship.

Now Euphemus, Poseidon's son – so sure-footed that it was said he could walk upon the water – made his way to the prow of the *Argo*, bracing strong legs to keep his balance. In one hand he held a small ring dove that he had been given by the Thracian King and had kept in a wooden cage under his rowing bench. The dove would serve as a decoy for the murderous rocks and give the men the time they needed to slide between them.

Euphemus loosed the bird. It fluttered for a moment, then flew straight toward the gap between the rocks. Sensing the dove's approach, they crashed together. The next moment, the men of the *Argo* saw her soar free – missing her tail feathers.

"Now!" cried the helmsman Tiphys, and the men bent to their oars. The rock mouth yawned ahead; the current sucked at the ship. Having been cheated of a victim, the Symplegades were angry. For a moment, as if through a window to another world, the Argonauts saw a wide, calm sea spread out beyond the barrier; then a great wave arose in the opening and blotted out the sight. With a shout, Tiphys turned the *Argo's* bow directly toward the wall of water. The prow, with its oak branch, rose up and up, impossibly up, until it seemed that the ship would plunge stern first down into the sea. But the wave rolled away under the ship's keel

Awaiting Jason and the Argonauts at the gateway to the Black Sea
were the rock giants known as the Symplegades, a pair of granitic monsters
forming a maw that could crush any ship to splinters.

They were in the passage now, and the blackened, rain-slick stone faces were rushing toward them.

Timbers quaking, the *Argo* sprang forward, riding up and over the furious swell, while blinding mist boiled and writhed around the seafarers. With a terrible roar, the Symplegades smashed together, grinding and shrieking after the concussion. But they missed their prey. The rocks had crushed the tip of the carved stern; that was all. The Argonauts had gained the inland sea.

Now the water was calm, and high above it a kingfisher soared, its wings like fire in the sunlight. Behind them, all was still. The Symplegades had ceased to move; they were closed together and skirted by ruffling foam. The Argonauts had done what no sailors had ever accomplished. Their feat fulfilled an ancient prophecy: that the Symplegades would remain forever fixed in place if a mortal-built ship passed safely between them.

But the passage had been accomplished only with divine help. The men later said that they had seen the giant figure of white-browed Athena rise from the waters as the huge wave grasped the ship; she had held the vessel—protected by the branch of her sacred oak—in the safety of her hand and carried it past the danger.

This was the exhilarating climax of the Argonauts' voyage. It was their single greatest triumph of seamanship—and the last achievement to be unspoiled by human treachery and strife. The Argonauts sailed on to Colchis, where Jason seduced the Colchian King's daughter Medea. Skilled in witchcraft, she helped the Greeks obtain the fleece and fled her homeland with them.

Perhaps because of this dishonor, the adventure disintegrated into tragedy and shame. As if the very seas were angry, contrary winds plagued the Greeks on their homeward voyage. In alien waters, some of the best and bravest perished.

What happened when the *Argo* at last reached home is a matter of dispute. Some chroniclers said that Jason presented the golden fleece to his uncle and then, for reasons no one knew, sailed peacefully away. Some said that he murdered Pelias with the aid of Medea's magic and was driven from the city by the King's outraged subjects. Most agreed that he eventually abandoned Medea and came to a shabby end in Corinth, old and alone, dreaming of the glories of his youth. It seemed that he kept his ship near him, for it was said that he beached it in Corinth and slept in its shade, only to die when a rotted timber fell from the bowsprit and crushed him. As for the ship, it was blessed, unlike its master. The valiant *Argo* so pleased the gods that they lifted it to the heavens, to sail transfigured over southern lands as a shining constellation.

That a wooden ship should enjoy a grander fate than the seamen who sailed it did not surprise the chroniclers of Jason's day. The gods were as capricious in their dealings with the fledgling human race as they were powerful. A man could be the greatest of heroes among his peers, and yet to the gods—even to the least of the gods—that man was as a plaything, a figure to be used like a puppet. Those who controlled the toy might shower blessings on this favorite or that, but the same fickle deities were just as likely to topple a poor mortal player at the height of his glory for the amusement of watching him fall. Or so it seemed to people like Jason, whose lives swung crazily between extravagant success and crushing defeat, with no discernible pattern.

Ancient minds saw that immortals were at work in all the elements, but nowhere so dramatically as on the sea. Their fickleness showed in fitful winds that shifted and dropped to bedevil a flapping sail. The gods vented anger in gales that pummeled ships and shore. Then the gods would relent, and patches of blue would spread among the spent and tattered clouds, smiles breaking through heaven's tears. However widely separated by climate, distance and tongue, most of the world's seafaring peoples interpreted the water's moods in this fashion.

While sea-deities were all of the same essence — descended from the watery abyss that had once engulfed the universe — they had different names and legends attached to them, depending on the lands and oceans over which they held sway. Most were envisioned as benefactors of humankind, in spite of their unpredictable nature. This was true from earliest antiquity, when Babylonians revered the amphibian god Ea as lord of the arts and a mentor of men. It was said that Ea stayed in the waters of the Persian Gulf at night but came ashore by day to instruct human-

kind in cultivation, in letters, and in the mastery of astronomy. In Indian oceans dwelled the fish-god Varuna, whose breath made the sailors' wind. The seas of Japan were the home of kindly Kompira, patron god of seamen; sailors wore his image close to their skin, and Japanese warships once cast coin-filled casks overboard when they passed Kompira's shrine at Kotohira. These offerings were picked up by fishermen and carried to the shrine, so that Japan's nautical defenses might remain strong.

Sometimes the characters of sea-deities were colored by the natures of the oceans where they reigned. The cold and severe waters of the northern seas, for example, harbored the forbidding Scandinavian gods Aegir and Ran, soul-eaters who collected the bodies of drowned mortals in their undersea kingdom. In contrast, the mercurial ways of the Greek sea-gods reflected the caprice of the warm Aegean itself — now blue and jeweled, presenting a calm and loving face to the overarching heavens, now a storm-wracked destroyer. The old gods who ruled those waters were as chaotic as creation itself.

They had a thousand names and more than a thousand faces, for they themselves were as fluid in form and character as their watery element. And as old: The father of all living things, said the Greeks, was Oceanus, manifest as a great stream girdling the world; the mother was Tethys, his consort. From these two sprang the Old Men of the Sea. Of them, the eldest was kindly Nereus, known in Jason's time by the appearances of his fifty lovely sea-nymph daughters, the Nereids, who often

Lashing the great white mares of the waves, the god of horses and lord of the ocean drove the swells in a golden chariot. Poseidon was this sea king's name.

were glimpsed playing among the waves, sea shells agleam in their streaming hair. Another was Phorcys, father of sea monsters. Yet another of the Old Men was Proteus, who might be seen on rocky islands, shepherding herds of seals. Proteus was the most elusive of creatures, for his shape changed constantly. He might appear as a man or a fish, or a flame upon the water, or only as spindrift hanging above the waves.

The ruler of them all was the sea-god Poseidon, son and conqueror of the most ancient race of gods, the Titans. Brother to Zeus, lord of the air, and to Dis, the underworld King, Poseidon could gather clouds and wind, raise or quiet waves, allow safe voyages through his world or doom the sailor. He was the father of sea storms, lord of flood, sender of earthquakes. Mortals believed that his palace lay in a shimmering cave deep within the Gulf of Euboea, east of the Greek mainland; they said he appeared on the waters in a chariot drawn by a hundred horses—white beasts with golden manes and hoofs of brass.

Poseidon was as fertile as the waters he ruled; hundreds of sea and island creatures were his children. Some were sea nymphs, fathered upon Nereids; one was the winged horse Pegasus, whose mother was

Medusa, the snake-headed Gorgon; some were half-human, begotten on mortal women. Some, such as the one-eyed giant Polyphemus, living alone in a Sicilian cave, were vicious monsters.

Nymph or horse, man or monster, they were proof of the endless fecundity of the sea. Poseidon's power sheltered them and punished rash mortals who dared to do them harm. It was no small thing to arouse the sea-god's wrath.

Of sailors who angered the god, the most famous was Odysseus, chieftain of Ithaca, a wily fighter in the army of Greeks who triumphed in the Trojan War. At that war's end, when Troy was a smoking ruin,

Odysseus set sail for home, commanding a convoy of twelve painted war galleys not much different from Jason's *Argo* of a generation before. The journey should have been a relatively straightforward affair. It involved sailing from Troy on the coast of what is now Asia Minor, south through the Cyclades, around the tip of the Peloponnesus, and up the western coast of Greece to Ithaca. Such a trip would normally be completed in a few weeks. Because of Poseidon, it took Odysseus ten years to reach home.

Odysseus was aptly named: The word was Greek for "victim of enmity." But he was no innocent victim of god or man.

Although he had courage and cleverness in abundance, he was merciless and a prince of liars. His men were worse. The years of encampment and fighting on Troy's windy plain had coarsened their honor and hardened their hearts. Careless of their gods, the Greeks invited their own disasters.

The sailors were still charged with battle lust when they left Troy. Instead of heading south, they steered north to the Thracian coast, intent on piracy. They sacked the city of Ismaros and slew almost all of its inhabitants. After the attack, the pall of smoke hanging over the shattered city could be seen for miles inland. The Greeks left with all the treasure they could stow under their rowing benches, but these spoils would cost them dearly. Evidently they had aroused some god's wrath, for no sooner had they made the open sea than a gale struck them. The ships' sails were shredded in the blasting wind, and the oars snapped.

So ferocious was the storm that Odysseus and his men were blown far to the south, into the cruel, uncharted seas that rimmed the world. Jason's course to Colchis can be followed on any map, but no chart showed the mist-shrouded realm where Odysseus wandered, a place where the oldest magics still lived and gods' children still played.

The seafarers might even then have gone home safely had not Odysseus struck against the sea-god himself. Leaving the larger part of his fleet in a safe haven, the warrior mounted a foray on Sicily—then a waste of tumbled rocks and meager pasture inhabited by the one-eyed giant shepherds called Cyclopes. Ever

the rogue, Odysseus stole the sheep and goats of one of them and blinded the giant with a stake through its single eye. Then he fled with his companions, carrying the animals to the ship.

Polyphemus, one of Poseidon's many sons, was the being they had brutalized. He lumbered behind the invaders, howling and snuffling at their scents as they made for their ship. But they loaded and launched the galleys before he could reach them. Arrogant in victory, Odysseus looked back at his victim and shouted his own name over the rising wind so that the Cyclops should know who had bested him. The giant knelt upon the rocky shore and called upon the god.

"Hear, Father," he screamed. "Grant that if my enemy Odysseus ever returns home, he may arrive late, in evil plight, from a foreign ship, having lost all his comrades."

Odysseus laughed. But Poseidon heard. No sooner had the captain rejoined his fleet than the sea shuddered under the ships, and the currents pulled at them.

From that time, Odysseus' voyage became a wandering from island to island and terror to terror. The longing for Ithaca and his own hearth grew strong in him, but longing was of little use against the hostility of the god. Tales were later told of an isle of cannibals who devoured Odysseus' men and smashed their beached ships with boulders; only Odysseus' ship, which the leader had anchored offshore, escaped destruction. Having a strong instinct for self-preservation, he fled at once across the unknown sea with his remaining men.

The lone vessel's next port was the Island of the Dawn, ruled by Circe, mother of witches. She turned the Greek men into rooting swine, and Odysseus was left companionless. Yet he escaped: He seduced the enchantress and ultimately fathered three children on her. At last she freed his people from their animal shapes. Circe agreed to let the Greeks go on with their wandering – on the condition that the leader prove his valor by sailing to the region of the dead at the last frontiers of the world, beyond the fogbound land of perpetual dusk.

Odysseus did this. In the land of the dead, in a thick-misted grove of black poplar and trailing willow, he sacrificed a ram and a black ewe, as the enchantress had instructed. The scent of the steaming blood drew flocks of thirsty ghosts, frail as shadows, whimpering like children. The first to appear was one of Odysseus' own men, killed on the voyage; Odysseus' mother was there, as were comrades who had fallen at Troy. All clustered, begging for ease, and Odysseus gave them blood to drink.

"A hardy man," Circe said, when Odysseus returned to her. "Most warriors find that one death journey is enough. The day will come when you will have taken two." She smiled her secret witch's smile and whispered words in his ear to guide him. Then she released him and his ragged company and summoned a wind to speed their galley on its way.

Circe sent the seafarers into danger, directing them toward the region where Poseidon ruled. But, playing fair, she had warned Odysseus of it. They had a day of peaceful sailing under a clear sky. Snowy clouds skimmed the air above them; bright fish leaped and danced around the ship, and the wrinkling waters glittered in their wake. Late in the day, when the westering sun made a path across the water, the wind dropped, and far ahead, the silhouette of an island came into view.

Then Odysseus did as the witch had told him. He had his sailors plug their ears with the beeswax used in sail mending, so that the only sound they heard was the pounding of their own pulses. Because he wished to hear the music he knew would soon begin, he had the men lash him to the mast for safety. The island ahead was the stronghold of sea Sirens, more seductive than any mortal woman, more murderous than any witch, thirstier for human blood than any poor shade.

The sailors rowed. Imprisoned by his bindings, Odysseus waited. The island silhouette grew larger. And over the water, light as dawn wind, a music started, a golden melody in which twined the loveliest of world sounds – the breathing of the calm sea, the whispering of water reeds, the sweet hiss of spring rain. As harmonies quivered in the air, Odysseus strained at his bonds, making no cry for fear of missing any of the music.

But when the ship approached the little island, Odysseus began to weep and scream and tear impotently at the bonds his men had made. Although the island was no more than a pile of rocks washed by the waves and littered with the bones and emptied skulls of sailors who had been this

Sea nymphs, singing songs that drove men mad with longing, sought to draw the adventurer
Odysseus into their deadly embrace. They were the Sirens, a name that meant "entanglers."

*Once-lovely Scylla, made into a six-headed man-eater by enchantment,
laired in coastal caves, hungry for seafarers. Those who escaped her jaws
risked being devoured by her partner, the whirling sea mouth Charybdis.*

way before, Odysseus did not see the place for a charnel house. The singers had come into view, and they were beautiful—more beautiful than any mortal woman, dearer-seeming than any wife or goddess. They sang and beckoned, and the mortal man's mind drowned in their pale eyes. He called and struggled. As if in answer, the Sirens leaped into the sea and played around the boat, hair streaming, white flesh glistening with water. Long fingers clutched at the gunwales, and the song filled all the air.

But the seamen rowed stolidly on. They could not hear the melodies of enchantment, and they had seen the litter of dead men's bones. Not until the women and their island had disappeared astern, not until their captain had stopped his struggles and lost his madness, did the men

dare to loosen his bonds and free him.

They left the Sirens' waters only to plunge into disaster. Their curious, shifting, dreamlike course had taken them from the unknown regions into the known, where age-old predators still lurked at the fringes of mortals' territory. The Strait of Messina, between the cliffs of the Italian mainland and the shore of Sicily, was haunted, and according to the chroniclers, the shipmates found themselves in those dark waters now. In mainland caves laired the six-headed sea monster Scylla, devourer of men; nearby in the waters of the strait lay the whirlpool called Charybdis, swallower of ships.

Rowing against a stiff headwind, the men pulled into the channel. They saw the seething pool to starboard almost at once. Charybdis did not always wake, but she had wakened now. Her feeding had just begun. As she sucked noisily at the sea, a flash of black sand and writhing, gasping fish showed at her core. Odysseus ordered the men to keep close

to the Italian coast. He did not mention Scylla, unseen behind her rocks. It was better to risk losing a few men than the entire ship and crew.

And that is what happened. The men strained through the narrow corridor, eyes fixed on the whirlpool, and Scylla struck viciously from the port side. Her claws raked the deck and fastened on sailors, hauling them into the air. She was enormous, her six heads slavering and barking. The hapless sailors dangled in her arms, crying piteously to their captain. Odysseus could do nothing but urge the rowers forward. Then Scylla settled back in her cave, cramming the men into long-toothed mouths, cracking their bones and crushing them into bloody pulp.

New horrors awaited the survivors. In the next days, storms blew up around them. A bolt of lightning flung from the heavens splintered the vessel, scattering flaming spars and planks across the water. Odysseus was the only man left alive. He clung to a section of mast and drifted for days under a blazing sun and cold, uncaring moon, until at last he beached on yet another of the islands strewn across the sea girdling the world. This was a sheltering place, graced by meadows where tall irises grew and stands of poplar and alder thickets hid the land from the sea. Here Odysseus rested—some said for five years, some for seven—in the company of the island's mistress, a daughter of Oceanus named Calypso. Her charms bound him to the secret place for a time, but they could not still his longing for his own kind. Day after day, he sat on the shore, staring across the sea, and at last Calypso released him

to once again brave the realm of Poseidon.

His vessel was no fine galley now, but a raft made from lashed-together trunks of trees and fitted with a mast and linen sail. Odysseus built it himself, with bronze tools Calypso gave him; he was a man who could turn his hand to any work.

All alone he made his way across the ocean, his hand always on the steering oar, for a lone sailor could not close his eyes long in sleep. At night he navigated by the close-set stars of the Pleiades and watched the Great Bear slowly wheel in place as it stared warily across the heavens at Orion the Hunter. In daylight he steered by the sun, always scanning the sea for danger. All he saw were endless ranks of swells stretching away to an empty horizon.

The man on the raft was no more than a mote in this watery vastness, but Poseidon spied him nevertheless. On the seventeenth day of the voyage, the god blew a fierce breath at Odysseus' back. It ripped the steering oar from his hand and curled the waves into claws that closed around him. Whitecaps broke over Odysseus' head, salt water burned in his throat and nostrils. With bursting lungs, he sank down into blackness.

Then, said the storytellers, the sea showed its caprice. A hand grasped Odysseus' arm and supported him so that his head rose above the water. Pale eyes looked for a moment into his own, and a voice spoke above the waves' roar. This was Leucothea, a goddess filled with pity for the sea's victims. She wound a veil of green around Odysseus' body to protect him. Thus armored with magic, he drifted easily with the current.

It took him to a forbidding shoreline, gray in the morning light and rising in sheer cliffs. Odysseus stood in the shallow water at their feet, trembling with cold and exhaustion. The green veil fell away and vanished. Then, step by shaking step, he felt his way along the wall of stone, searching for some gateway to the land. It would be cruel to have survived the deep only to die face-down in the shallows.

He came at length to a narrow gap in the cliffs and stumbled through it onto a rocky stream bed; here, fresh waters ran down to the sea. Along the bubbling path Odysseus lurched, until he reached a place where grass grew on the stream bank and a willow copse hugged the verge, trailing long branches in the water. There Odysseus heaved himself onto dry land. He was naked, but this was of no account. He crawled among the willows and, in their shelter, fell to the ground, asleep almost as soon as his head touched the grass.

A splash awoke him. Confused, he stared up at the canopy of leaves, flickering yellow-green in the sunlight of late afternoon. Rolling over, he peered out from his shelter. A leather ball floated in the water of the stream. On the bushes nearby fluttered shapes of white—tunics and blankets and bed linens, spread out to dry in the sun. And dancing along the grass toward the water were women—not pale sea nymphs or dark island enchantresses, but pretty, rosy women of his own race. They were laughing as they ran. It was they, he saw, who had washed the linen that hung by the stream and they who played at ball while they waited for the clothing to dry. They were so healthy, so gay and safe and carefree that Odysseus' heart turned over; their very laughter sang to him of home.

He covered his nakedness with a leafy branch and went to meet them. The women stared. The younger ones backed away timidly and ducked their heads and giggled, but a tall maiden advanced and gravely said, "Greetings, stranger from the sea."

"You see me before you, sweet lady, a shipwrecked sailor far from home," said Odysseus. "What is this place? Where may I find shelter?"

Even gaunt and naked, with seaweed clinging in his beard, Odysseus could charm. The maiden smiled and said, "This place is the island of Drepane, ruled by the Phaeacians. I am Nausicaa, daughter of the King, and I will take you to him." She signaled her maidens to gather the washing. Then the company headed across the grass and onto a road that led to the painted palace of the Phaeacian King.

Within its gate Odysseus was made welcome as a hearth guest. He was led to bathing chambers and clothed and fed, and no one asked his name. In the hall of the King that night, Nausicaa sang of the battle of Troy and of the heroes who shone there; Achilles she named, and Patroclus, Achilles' friend, and lumbering Ajax and clever Odysseus.

The song died. "I am Odysseus, who fought at Troy," said the hearth guest. "I

Cast into the waves when a wrathful Poseidon shattered his ship, Odysseus
received unexpected aid from another divinity of the sea. Leucothea, the white
goddess, rose from the waters and offered him the shelter of her enchanted veil.

am old now, and my beard is gray, but I remember well the ventures of my youth." The siege of Troy had begun twenty years ago; it had lasted ten years, and Odysseus, cursed by Poseidon, had wandered for ten years after. He was bent, it was true, but not beaten—and Odysseus had a silver tongue. For hours, while King and company listened as closely as children and the fires sank low, the warrior told them tales of his youth.

They did him honor for it. The heroes of Troy had been sung for a decade: They were the most valiant of Greeks. The Phaeacian King, whose name was Alcinous, offered any boon, and Odysseus asked for passage home.

It was given most sumptuously. Alcinous provided a handsome galley and a crew to sail it. He sent Odysseus southeast from Drepane, down the Greek coast to Ithaca. Exhausted, his wandering at an end, the old warrior slept through the days of the voyage; he did not even stir when the galley ground onto the Ithacan shore. The Phaeacians carried him to land and laid him within an olive grove to sleep his fill, and then they made for home. But they had not reckoned on the rage of Poseidon. At the entrance to their home harbor, ship and crew were changed into stone by the sea-god who had been cheated of his prey.

As for Odysseus, he returned home in just the manner Poseidon's son had demanded—bereft of all his comrades, carried on a foreign ship, and in an evil plight. He was penniless; he was aged. He was not even recognized at first, so much had he changed, and he found his lands overrun by rebellious men, all of them vying for the hand of his wife, since he was presumed to have died. He fought them valiantly and, in the end, regained his wife and the rule of Ithaca.

But death came to Odysseus at last. According to one account, a stranger raided Ithaca, as Odysseus himself had raided islands in his younger years. The old man set out to fight the interloper and was killed on the beach by a spear tipped with a sting ray's barb. The youth who killed him was his own son, the man-child the island enchantress Circe had borne him.

That Odysseus should die beside the waters that washed his land was only fitting. In that maritime nation long ago, the sea-gods ruled. In time, however, mortals—ever growing in strength—lost sight of the powers that had repeatedly reminded men like Odysseus and Jason of their smallness. A day would come, long distant, when humankind would no longer perceive the gods at work in shipwrecks and whirlpools and death by water. The old deities would be celebrated not with burnt offerings and libations, but only in songs and tales.

Yet the perils they offered did not abate over the years. The slender galleys of the Greeks might be dwarfed by the massive vessels of later ages, but even those sturdy ships were not proof against the forces of wind and wave. And there were other dangers, too, lurking deep within the age-old seas, waiting for mortal trespassers who strayed too far from shore.

Predators from the Primal World

Seafarers sought to master the ocean and drive away its spirits, but powerful survivors of the first ages of creation long lurked on empty shores and in the deeps. Immeasurably old, filled with wrath, these beasts became the stuff of seamen's tales.

Thus northern mariners sang of serpents lairing in icy caves, scanning for ships with keen eyes. Such a creature's attack was swift and silent. Before they died, its victims saw only a ripple in the waters, a swaying head above a mast and a gaping mouth eager for flesh.

A Pelagic Scavenger

When they spoke of monsters, ancient chroniclers named Tiburon. It had a shark's teeth, sharp as scimitars, but no shark could match its size. Large as a small frigate, it followed in the wake of sailing ships far from land, and left no hope for seamen swept overboard. No line could save those hapless men. Tiburon fed on them, and his belly became their grave.

A Spinner of Maelstroms

Woe to the seafarers who
beheld Leviathan. A creature
so vast that it dwarfed
the largest whale, it kept
for the most part to the
valleys of the sea floor.
When hunger brought it to
the surface, however, sailors
were lost, the stories said. Its
lashing fins and tail created
maelstroms that sucked
whole ships down to its cold
and sunless realm.

A Tentacled Invader

Almost soundlessly, always stealthily, the Devil Fish invaded the very hearts of sailing ships with slippery and many-suckered tentacles. Through hatchways and portholes, the octopoid arms would slide, searching out flesh for the Devil Fish to feed on. It killed by crushing; axes and knives severed tentacles, but each attack dragged a few luckless seamen from the safety of their vessels.

Chapter Three

Wraiths of Wind and Wave

Contrary to many landsmen's beliefs, it is not the dogwatch, from four to eight at night, that sailors hate; it is the midwatch, from midnight to four in the morning. These are long hours, slow and unchanging, when the seaman's only company is wind and wave, when his shipmates sleep below, when his own strength is at its lowest ebb. Disaster can strike then, borne on the night wind and carried by the changing tide. The midwatch is the time when the sea gives up its dead:

On a night in March, long years ago, herring were running on Dogger Bank – the shallow, sandy-bottomed waters in the North Sea between England and Denmark – and several British fishing ships were anchored there, waiting for the light. Among them was the *Maria*, a handsome schooner out of Hull; the smaller *Speedwell*, out of Whitby, lay nearby. In the small hours of the night, a gale tore down from the north with the running spring tide. Under the force of the shrieking gusts, the anchor lines of the *Maria* parted. She swept down on the little *Speedwell* and plowed into her amidships. The *Maria* was hardly damaged, but the *Speedwell*, a great hole torn in her side, listed, took sea after savage sea over her decks, and sank. Although the captain of the *Maria* mounted a search once he had his ship under control, he found no survivors.

The *Maria* returned to Hull for repairs late the following day, and tension was rife among the crew. Some of them said the captain had blood on his hands, for it was his ship that had wrought destruction in the darkness. These crewmen left his service. Nevertheless, he took the *Maria* out again as soon as she was seaworthy, and early one evening about a month after the accident, he dropped anchor once more at Dogger Bank.

The April night was fine and promised a finer day. Stars glittered, remote and silver in the heavens. When the new moon rose, its horns were pointed up, so that it seemed to be a bowl from which water could not spill – the seaman's sign that the weather would be dry. As night zephyrs stirred, the halyards slapped lightly against the masts, and the water whispered around the hull. There was no other sound, except for the occasional sighs and groans any wooden ship makes.

At midwatch, the deck glimmered in the darkness. The horn lantern hanging on the foremast cast a pool of yellow light, and in the shadows glowed intermittent red pinpoints of seamen's pipes. The men watched the stars and thought their private thoughts. Then something moved in the water, took shape in the air. The sailors stared.

Rising from the sea all around the ship were the figures of men: pale men whose faces glistened with water and whose clothes hung in tattered, dripping rags; silent men whose dark eye sockets were fastened on the schooner *Maria*. They hovered just above the surface of the water, wavering like candle flames. Then, one by one, they rose. White-fingered hands fumbled at the gunwales. The figures heaved themselves over the railings and soundlessly took up seamen's stations, their faces empty and blind. A man drifted to the wheel; his hands moved easily over it, as if he were steering, but the wheel did not turn. In the bow, sliding in and out of the nimbus of the lantern, other men unwound nets that were not there and cast them out into the sea. Working in rhythm, they hauled the nets in, straining at the lines, but no fish flopped onto the *Maria's* decks.

Hour after hour, while the living men watched, rigid with fear, the dead men plied their trade. Only when the first faint pinkness showed in the eastern sky did they cease. The figures trembled and faded; they flowed like streams of water over the railings and dropped into the sea without a splash, vanishing from view.

As if released from a trance, the men of the watch stirred at last. They called for the captain and told what they had seen. He shrugged and sent them about their business. He forced his crew to work that

day, and when the time came, he himself took the midwatch. So he saw the ghost crew; he knew them for what they were but would not say it.

His men said it, however. These were the ghosts of the men of the *Speedwell*, which now lay below them in the sands of Dogger Bank. Unburied, they were restless, for it was the *Maria* that had sent them to the bottom. Her passage through the waters above was the call that brought them to the surface.

Eventually, the captain took the *Maria* back to Hull, and there he lost his crew. He found another, but when he took them out to fish the Dogger Bank, the spectral company appeared once more. After that, fewer and fewer men would sail with him. Even the most pitiable of waterfront wretches declined when offered a berth on the *Maria*, and in the end the captain left her permanently moored at Hull. What became of him the storytellers did not report. As for the *Maria*, she rotted away at her moorings and at last sank ignominiously into the depths.

Such hauntings were common once; tales of sea ghosts were told by sailors everywhere, and these ghosts were more feared than any monster, for they were said to be harbingers of death. That is why the men of Hull refused to ship with the schooner *Maria*. No seaman cared to view his own mortality.

On the waters of the globe, death was never very far away. Even after the seagods dwindled into legend, sailors sensed that they were at the mercy of forces beyond human understanding. When seamen ventured onto the deep, natural magic lay all around. They skimmed the surface of a vast and unknown territory and saw there manifestations of the secret life below: The sea was the most changeable of beings. The winds might sing sweetly behind the sailors and the currents push them along; then, for reasons no one could fathom, perverse winds might blow for weeks on end and currents turn contrary. Or worse, the ships could lie motionless for days, painted toy boats fixed to a gleaming mirror that doubled the withering rays of the sun.

Everywhere, peril waited patiently. A seaman might die from starvation; scurvy might drain his strength; his ship might perish in fire. Off the coast of Newfoundland, mountain-sized icebergs lurked unseen in fog banks. North of Norway, colliding currents made a vicious whirlpool called the Maelstrom, and by the Scottish coast spun another whirlpool known simply as "The Hag." (It was said by the old wives in the shore villages to have been home to Celtic sea-gods.) Around the great capes of the Southern Hemisphere, westerly winds blowing across a fetch of thousands of miles of open water created seventy-foot waves that could overwhelm any ship. And these were only a few of the terrors of the sea.

Death by water was a terrible death: The sea's cold fingers clutched the sailor, dragging him into its unloving arms, darkening his mind and filling his lungs with pain. Sailors believed that the sea demanded lives. So strong was their conviction that few of them even learned to swim, explaining that a quick death was better than one that came after hours of struggle against the indomitable power of the sea. And some folk—landsmen and seafarers alike—were afraid to rescue the drowning: Cheated of one life, the waters would seek another.

And so the end was a bed on the cold ocean floor, far from the sunlight, where the body rolled and swayed in underwater breezes, where fish nibbled on the sailor's eyes, lobsters plucked at the flesh of his feet and branching coral rooted in his bones. Seafarers called this grave Davy Jones's Locker. Some thought that "Davy" was a corruption of the word "duffy"—African slaves' patois for "ghost"—and that "Jones" derived from the Biblical Jonah, who was sacrificed to the sea by sailors anxious to escape a storm. Others speculated the term descended from the name of the Hindu goddess of death—Deva Lokka. But no one knew for certain.

Those who sailed upon the deep understood its power and defended against it as best they could, in the building and launching of their ships and in the management of them. In northern countries, for instance, keels were laid on consecrated ground—a place dedicated to the old gods or, in later days, to the Christian one. Building was begun on an auspicious day. In pagan times, that was invariably Wednesday, the day sacred to the supreme god Woden and bearing his name. Later, worship of Woden was forgotten, but many good Christian shipbuilders still laid their keels on Wednes-

Rooted to the ocean floor, never sleeping, never free, drowned sailors rocked in the current,
their bodies prey to sea creatures, their souls haunting the surface and begging for ease.

The ghosts of sailors drowned in the deep might appear on passing ships, clinging to the shrouds and clutching at the yardarms. The sight of them brought terror, for they came to call the living to watery graves.

days – not on Thursdays, named for Thor, god of storms; not Fridays, called after Freya, who led the Valkyries, gatherers of human souls. Shipbuilders also wanted a day when the sun shone and the good west wind blew; in the interest of the vessel's strong and steady growth under their hands, they wanted a time of month when the moon was waxing or full, not waning; and they wanted an hour when the tide was rising, not ebbing.

The old shipwrights used good wood – and for centuries favored the same woods, partly because of the quality of the timber and partly in memory of the sanctity of certain trees. Oak, once worshipped by Norsemen, Gauls, Greeks and Romans alike and thought to be a protection against lightning, was a primary choice, as was pine, once dedicated to the sea-gods. Trim could be apple – so revered in early times that a man could lose his life for felling the tree – or holly, long thought a protection against evil. Black walnut was never used: It was said to be the devil's tree and a lightning attractor.

The hull of a ship, when complete, was provided with painted *oculi*, or eyes, at the bow; these warded off malevolent magic. In later days, the painted *oculi* might be replaced with a carved figurehead – the soul of the ship – whose staring eyes offered the same protection. If the figurehead was of a woman, she was frequently bare-breasted, in memory of the ancient belief that a storm would give way to calm if a woman showed herself naked to it.

And when the ship was ready to be named and launched, the shipwrights chose a day as fine as that when the keel was laid. They prayed that flocks of gulls would circle overhead, for these were the friendly souls of dead sailors, and their cries were a benediction. Launching ceremonies were a sanguinary affair in early times: The Vikings spattered their ships with the blood of human sacrifice, the Greeks with animal blood. In the Christian era, a ship was blessed by a priest and christened with wine; then, quivering and rumbling, it slid over its launching rollers into the sea. After launch, however, Christian believers often made offerings to the ancient spirits. When the final fittings were completed, master builders placed silver coins beneath the mast steps as tithes to the winds.

That was only the beginning of the solicitation of divine aid or efforts to avert divine wrath. The men who sailed the ships of old – fishermen, merchants, explorers – surrounded themselves with protections against death by drowning. Best safeguarded was the man born with a caul – the thin membrane that sometimes covers newborn babies' heads. The caul would be carefully saved, and when that baby grew up and went to sea, he would keep it by him, because as long as he had it, the ship that carried him never would sink. Other safeguards included golden earrings in sailors' ears, iron horseshoes under the deck, and brooms nailed to the mast to sweep in good winds.

The rules regulating behavior and objects on board ship were another form of armament against the hazards of the sea. Orderliness was important, not only for

No footsteps were left by a woman who walked the Cornish coast by night. She was a ghost, tormented by grief, eternally searching for an infant who had died offshore.

efficiency, but because breaks in physical order opened gaps for cosmic disorder. No one whistled on ship—except possibly in a flat calm—because whistling was the oldest of means for calling up winds.

In Scotland and other places, certain animals and people were anathema on board: pigs, perhaps because they once had been associated with discarded pagan rites; hares, weasels and foxes, because they were the forms that witches—the sailors' enemies—could take; salmon, for reasons no one knew. So strong was the feeling about these creatures that Scottish sailors referred to them only by euphemisms. The pig was "the cold iron beastie," because if it were accidentally named, a Scotsman would touch cold iron—protection against enchantment. A salmon was called "the gentleman."

As for passengers, sailors were uneasy with women on board. And they preferred not to carry clergymen, as if the presence of the advocates of new celestial powers might arouse the anger of the old ones.

Above all, no dead man could be transported on a ship; the presence of a coffin was enough to cause mutiny, and sea captains knew it well. The corpse, the physical reminder of the fate of humankind, drew the baleful stare of eternity to the seafarers who companioned it. Its presence could cause storms at sea and killing fogs and rogue waves that came out of nowhere to tumble a ship to her doom. When the dead were near, the sea desired them, and sailors gave the corpses directly to the waters.

The burial was performed in a fashion that guarded against haunting. The dead man, washed and dressed, was sewed into a canvas shroud by the ship's sailmaker, who passed the last stitch through the corpse's nose to keep him in the shroud. Shot or shackles were chained to his feet so that he would sink—and so that he never could free himself to ascend from the sea bed to haunt the living. Then the sailors gathered aft; the ship hove to; the corpse was placed upon a plank and slipped into the water. In token of mourning—and perhaps to release the soul from the bonds of life—ceremonial disorder marked the hour of the passage: The yards were cockbilled—trimmed to lie at a curious angle to the deck—and line ends were left uncoiled.

Even if a seaman was properly committed to the deep, the circumstances of his death might preclude any real rest. The ghosts of those who died by drowning or murder or in warfare often drifted about for centuries, a torment to the living and a sign of impending disaster. Many of them lingered in the waters where they died, attracted to the surface by passing ships, as the men of the *Speedwell* were. The sight of their pale faces and dripping bodies rising from the waves or clinging to yardarms chilled the hearts of all who saw them, because they were the sea's sign that it wanted fresh bodies. Storm winds or some other natural assault soon followed.

Some ghosts haunted the shore rather than the pelagic realm. In a few cases, these pathetic wraiths owed their condition to the loss of a loved one to the sea. For example, on the beaches of Saint Ives in Cornwall, when winter

A fiery portent

Before storms at sea, when the air brimmed with electricity, spirit fires played in the rigging of sailing ships, flying from mast to mast and top to top, and sailors saw in them portents of the future. They said that if only one light leaped in the rigging, the ship was heading toward stormy death; if two shone, the winds would lull and the seas quiet. Or they said that descending flames meant disaster, and ascending ones fair weather. Some seafarers thought the lights were ghosts of old comrades come to warn of perils; all believed that if the lights played on a living man's head, that man was doomed.

So familiar was the phenomenon that sailors gave it names. Some called the light St. Elmo's fire, the name being a corruption of Erasmus, the Syrian patron saint of sailors. The Greeks named it the Dioscuri, for the Argonaut twins Castor and Polydeuces, who guarded the souls of seafaring men after death. And the Portuguese called the lights corposants – or "bodies of saints" – believing they were the spirits of the blessed.

chilled the land, a wanderer might see a lantern light glimmering through the sheets of icy rain; it marked the ghost of a woman who had been shipwrecked there. Although she had been pulled from the water, the infant she carried in her arms had been sucked into the tide. She died of grief. Ever after, her sad ghost wandered in search of the child.

In the Hebrides, fishermen refused to set foot on the island of Scarba after dusk. High-cliffed and forbidding, Scarba was stalked by hundreds of sailor phantoms whose hellish howls echoed far out over the evening sea and whose twisted, shuffling shapes showed as shadows when the moonlight glistened on the island's deadly rocks. North German coastal villages were prey to *Gongers*, the ghosts of the drowned, who appeared at twilight, leaving pools of water on the stones and sands where they walked. In Denmark, spirits haunted lonely beaches; the Danes called them *strand varsler*, or "the coast guard."

Such spirits were well known in every kingdom, and in some countries they were feared not because they were the dead calling the living to their doom, but because they were themselves destructive. Jealous of the warm existence of humanity, these spirits laid cold, cruel hands on men and women, sometimes killing and sometimes maiming.

Ghosts such as these plagued the coastal waters of Japan's mist-shrouded, island-studded Inland Sea for many centuries, drifting ashore near the western tip of Honshu. They were the unliving survivors of an earlier period of history when rival warrior families battled for empire. In those days, warlords of the Taira clan held the country in an iron grip; they had purged the Inland Sea of pirates and established a kind of sullen peace across the land before they were driven west across Honshu by the soldiers of the Minamoto family. The Taira moved toward the sea with their Emperor, who was only a small boy. They fought in the forests and in the hills and on the shores of Honshu. Then they built a flotilla and took to the Inland Sea. The Minamoto followed, and warriors in thousands of small boats battled in the coastal area called Dan-no-ura. In the end, the Taira perished; the little Emperor drowned in his grandmother's arms, and the Minamoto began a rule that was to last for hundreds of years.

But the Taira remained where they had fallen. So pervasive was their presence that even the crabs that scuttled the sands at Dan-no-ura carried marks resembling human faces on their backs and were called ghosts of the Taira. The real ghosts, however, manifested themselves as tongues of fire hovering over the waves and on the beaches, or as voices shouting battle cries over the sea in the dark hours of the night. So terrifying were these phantoms of the waters that the shore people built a temple called Amidaji at the extreme southwestern tip of Honshu and surrounded it with stone monuments inscribed with the names of the drowned boy Emperor and his people. The air was quieter after that, but the Taira had not vanished. They lay invisible, awaiting the call of living voices that would rouse them

Centuries ago, the warriors of the Minamoto family fought the ruling clan of the Taira
in the strait that guarded Japan's Inland Sea. The Taira lost all earthly power there,
staining the waves with blood. But their ghosts still haunted the living on nearby shores.

from their sleep. Sailors knew not to speak the names of the dead, but some landsmen were unaware of the danger.

A temple priest named Hoichi summoned the Taira all unknowing. He was old and blind, but he had earned fame for his poetry and his skill on the four-stringed lute. He sang tales of the Taira and the Minamoto, recounting their deeds of glory and identifying their heroes.

One summer night, Hoichi sat alone on the veranda that surrounded his temple. The air was heavy with the scents of jasmine and lily; crickets chirped in the garden, and tree frogs filled the air with their twinkling songs. Hoichi plucked at his lute from time to time, bringing forth the plaintive cry peculiar to the instrument. But for the most part, he was content to listen, drawing images from the night noises around him, in the manner of the blind.

Then a deep, stern voice called Hoichi's name. He raised his head and said, "I do not see you, for I am blind, but I answer."

Heavy footsteps shook the wooden planking of the veranda; a heavy hand fell on Hoichi's shoulder.

"My lord summons you, priest, to sing of the battle of Dan-no-ura. He waits with his people now."

Obediently, Hoichi rose from his place and followed where his summoner led. The man said not a word as he guided the priest, but the sounds he made were the sounds of a warrior—the dull clink of armor, the harsh whisper of silk.

After they had walked some distance, the warrior paused and cried "Open!" A gate creaked. The two men moved on. Around them, marching footsteps drummed and stopped; ahead of them, wooden screens thumped open. Hoichi was led into a chamber large enough to echo with the murmuring of many people. He sank to a cushion on the floor. A lute was put into his hands.

At once the whisperings and the rustlings of the crowd ceased. Grave attention settled on Hoichi. "Sing, priest, of the sorrows of Dan-no-ura," the deep voice commanded.

Hoichi sang a chanting song, rich with the magic of the poet. From the lute came the sea melody of oars stroking the water and bows slicing through the waves. The instrument spoke of battle—warriors yelling, arrows hissing in the air. He sang of the Emperor perishing in the water, and his lute wept for the child.

When he halted, he was greeted with a wailing sigh. A woman bent over him and touched him with a cool, soft hand. "The song pleases, poet," she said. "Leave us now and return tomorrow night. Tell no one of this place." He smiled at that. How could a blind man in unknown territory tell where he had been?

So the silent warrior led Hoichi back to his temple. The next night, the warrior returned. As if entranced, Hoichi rose and followed him and sang for the company once more. He returned obediently a third night, but then the pattern changed.

He sang his first chant and his second, and the company listened as before. When Hoichi plucked the notes for his third poem, however, hard hands seized him; his lute was pulled away; shouts echoed all around him. He struggled, but it was no use; he was dragged across rough ground, then grass, and then he knew no more.

He awoke to the familiar scents of his own temple and his own straw mats and the voices of his fellow priests. They grew hushed when he stirred.

"What is this?" Hoichi asked, sitting up. "Did you drag me thus roughly from the lord's house where I made my songs?"

After a moment, one of the priests said, "We followed you where you went. It is no lord's house you played in, Brother. You sat in the cold night air among the monuments, and a company of tall flames danced around you while you sang."

"Ah," Hoichi said.

There was no more to say. His singing of their names had called the Taira from the sea, and he was in their hands. They would be thirsty for his life soon, and they would drag him into the waters where their bodies lay.

His fellows loved him, however, and they set to work to save him. They stripped the old man. With long writing brushes, using the sweeping strokes of master craftsmen, they inscribed on his flesh the characters of protective texts that would hide him from the ghosts. The writings covered his breast, his back, his legs, his arms, even the palms of his hands and soles of his feet.

"When you are summoned again," they told him, "speak no word and make no move and so you will be hidden. If they do not find you, they lose their power and must go back to the sea."

Night came, and he sat again on his veranda, visionless and invisible, his dear lute in his lap for company. He did not move; he hardly breathed as he awaited the ghost's summoning voice.

"Hoichi!"

The warrior was just below him, in the garden. Hoichi made no sound. The commanding cry came again. Then the steps of the veranda creaked. Armor clinked beside him as the ghost squatted down.

"Where is the player? Here is a lute but no man is with it," a voice said softly in his ear.

The whisper died to a hiss, "I see no man. He is protected. No arms, no fine poet's hands, no priest's bare feet. I see only two ears, floating in the air, and these I claim for my lord."

Still Hoichi made no sound. He did not cry out, even when long, sharp nails dug deep into his ears and tore the flesh from his head; he did not weep as the blood dripped onto his shoulders and the footsteps faded away. In the distance, among the stone monuments, howling swelled and slowly died.

And when the moon rose, his fellow priests surrounded him. He was safe now from the banished ghosts—alive and whole except for his ears, which had not been touched by the priests' protective brushes and therefore had been visible and vulnerable to the ghost.

Ever after, he was called Mimi-nashi Hoichi, or "Hoichi the Earless." When he eventually died and was buried by his brother priests, he rested peacefully. His

Across the sea one night came the Cornish murderess Sarah Polgrain, a
shade pursuing with cold eyes and arms the sailor whose lover she had been in life.

fate could have been much worse. Those taken by sea ghosts joined their sleepless company. Like the family of the Taira or the phantoms of the isle of Scarba, like all the army of the night sea, they were doomed to drift in the deep or wander in the dark salt air, blown through spume and spindrift by the winds that moaned across the waters, lost to the light that warmed the living and to the sleep that eased the buried dead.

Such a one haunted the seas of Cornwall during the last century. In life he had been a fine, carefree young man, a sailor known in the taverns of Penzance as Yorkshire Jack: He had the glossy black hair and bright blue eyes often seen in northern counties. They attracted the attention of a bold and handsome young woman from the village of Ludgvan, whose name was Sarah Polgrain. The two were seen together through the months of one summer, walking the meadows near the village, Jack's dark head bent to Sarah's golden one. Although Sarah was married, she made no attempt at concealment. Her husband was elderly and frail and afraid of her sharp tongue.

Then Polgrain died. Sarah put it about the little village that he had succumbed to cholera, and the village doctor who examined him agreed that this was so. The old man was buried.

Sarah wept for her husband openly, but Ludgvan was a small place. Those of her neighbors who had passed near her house and heard her bullying her husband, and those who had seen her walking with her lover shook their heads and whispered. Rumor flowed in the narrow lanes of Ludgvan and lingered at the village well until, at last, Polgrain's body was exhumed. The corpse proved to be riddled with arsenic. Young Sarah was tried and found guilty of murder.

The crowd at the gallows was given a show. There stood Sarah over the trap, jaunty to the end. Her little shoes had curving heels; her beribboned dress was tucked up to show the flounces of her petticoat and the green stockings that she was wearing. Around her neck sat the hangman's noose, tied with thirteen turns for the thirteen disciples of Christ and wound withershins — counterclockwise — to attract the devil and send Sarah more quickly to hell. She held her head high, as if the noose were a fine necklace, and her eyes scanned the clusters of neighbors to find her lover, Yorkshire Jack.

He was there. Slowly he walked toward the gallows while the hangman waited. Muttering, the crowd made a path for him. He took Sarah in his arms. She whispered a moment, and all heard him reply, "I will." He kissed her and turned away. Sarah gave a smile and a wink to her neighbors. Then the hangman did his work.

The sailor changed after that. He seemed to waste away. Day by day he became thinner and paler. His hands trembled: "She follows me," he told his shipmates. "I promised to marry her because I thought she was mad, and now she will not let me go."

The sailors shook their heads; but the villagers of Ludgvan were not surprised. Sarah had been seen twice after the hanging, once loitering about the churchyard and once, at dusk, on the high road that led to the neighboring town.

When he went to sea again, Yorkshire Jack grew morose. He was frightened, and his fear spread through the crew. The forecastle of the merchantman, where the men's hammocks were slung, became a silent, sullen place. Yorkshire Jack kept apart. His shipmates ascribed this to the presence of a companion; they could not see her, but they could feel her there, as strong as she had been in life and as patient as the grave.

After a voyage of some weeks, the ship returned home, sailing back into the waters of Mounts Bay. And it was there, one night just before the midwatch, that Sarah Polgrain summoned Yorkshire Jack. Every man in the forecastle heard her. Above the creaking of the hammocks and the sighing of the ship came the sound of little heels tapping along the deck, coming closer, moving unerringly in the darkness to the corner where Jack lay. His fellows turned their heads, but saw only shadow. The young man gave a bleak and weary sigh. He heaved himself up and went out to the deck, accompanied by the merry tapping of little heels.

The end was swift. Jack made for the bulwarks. He climbed them and, without a backward glance, leaped into the sea. The watch saw him go. In the dark water, his pale face floated for a moment; beside it appeared another, just as pale.

That was the last of Yorkshire Jack. His shipmates swore that bells tolled under Mounts Bay at the moment the waters closed over the companioned heads. They – and others after them – heard Jack's voice wailing through the sea sounds, "I will, I will, I will."

So Yorkshire Jack joined the spectral company of the sea. Like most others of his kind, his shade seemed confined to the place where his body was drowned, and he haunted only those who sailed the waters above his bones.

Sometimes, however, apparitions ranged widely on the oceans of the world. The most famous and feared of these roving phantoms was borne on his journeys by the ship that had carried him in life. Sometimes the ghost vessel loomed out of the night without warning, all sails set and heading toward collision, only to vanish into the air; sometimes it seemed a ship of fire; sometimes its sailors could be seen, a crew of tattered skeletons. It terrified the men who spied it, for in its wake came storm and disease and madness.

Even the dry words entered in a ship's log could not disguise the fear the ghost ship wrought, as a report from the last century attests. On a night in July, during the midwatch, a British ship sighted the demon vessel:

"She first appeared as a strange red light," wrote the captain, "as of a ship all aglow, in the midst of which light, her masts, spars and sails, seemingly those of a normal brig, some two hundred yards distant from us, stood out in strong relief as she came up. Our lookout on the forecastle reported her close to our port bow, where also the officer of the watch from the bridge clearly saw her, as did our quar-

This was a sight to chill a seaman's heart: the Flying Dutchman, speeding before her own
ghost wind and crewed by a company of the dead. She augured death to those who spied her.

Forever lashed by wind and rain, forever braced on a rolling deck, the
spectral captain of the Flying Dutchman sailed his ship wherever sea roads led.

terdeck midshipman who was sent forward at once to the forecastle to report back."

But the vessel vanished as the British ship approached her. That same day, the man who had first seen the fiery brig fell from the fore-topmast crosstree to the deck and was instantly killed. He was buried at sea in the afternoon. The captain's hour would come later. When he reached his home port, he discovered that he had a fatal illness.

The ghost ship was known to sailors of every nation, and many stories explain its genesis. The clearest account tells why it was called the *Flying Dutchman.*

A Dutch shipmaster named Vanderdecker was its last captain. Ruthlessly committed to speed, he was the kind of tyrant that seamen called a "lion." He would lock his passengers belowdecks while he hunted hurricanes to send his ship along; he would padlock the halyards to prevent any of his crew from shortening sail, even in the fiercest blow.

He met his fate near the notorious headlands of the Cape of Good Hope. A roaring wind blocked his approach to the Cape. Faced with the option of tacking far out to sea or close to shore, he chose to skirt the rocks. His crew protested, but Vanderdecker, excited by their fear, howled with laughter and held his course. A crewman tried to restrain him. He shoved the man overboard.

At this point, says the tale, a figure appeared on the quarterdeck. It may have been Adamastor, a ghost said to haunt the Cape, seeking human souls. Various reports described this specter as enormous, bearded, hollow-eyed and grim. It was he who brought killer storms to the Cape and he who spread over the tops of the headlands the ominous clouds called the "Devil's Tablecloth."

Whatever the phantom's identity, Vanderdecker screamed his defiance. The foremast snapped, then, and crashed to the deck. Above the wind, a banshee voice rang out and named the doom of the man who defied the sea. Vanderdecker was accursed, the spirit said. He would sail forever without rest or anchorage or port of any kind; he would always be on watch; he would be the evil of the sea, traveling all latitudes without the chance of repose. And his ship would bring misfortune to all who sighted it.

Vanderdecker drew his pistol and shot at the creature. The spirit did not move, but at the noise of the firing, the wind dropped, and the ghost vanished. Vanderdecker gazed around his vessel then. The foremast lolled crazily, the sails shuddered helplessly – dead things among the dead. His crew lay all about him, every man lifeless; and even as Vanderdecker stared at them, the flesh melted from their bones, leaving only skeletons to keep him company.

Then, solitary on the wide sea, forever denied any sailing man's comfort, the Dutchman stood to the wheel. He called for a wind; it rose at his command and filled the sails, although the sea that surrounded him remained flat calm. He set off into eternity, mortal no more. Of all the sea ghosts, he was the saddest, ever alone, ever feared, ever hated.

Rendezvous with a Death Ship

Not every vessel that ranged the seas steered its course to a living helmsman's hand. Ships of the dead also sailed, driven to and fro by forces no mortal mariner could comprehend. Such ships were inimical to the living; the very sight of them, it was said, portended death. Yet two men boarded a ghost ship once and lived to tell the tale.

They were Spaniards, a merchant and his servant, homeward bound across the Atlantic from Cuba. West of the Azores, on a night of howling winds, their vessel foundered, and the two men were swept into the monstrous waves. They grabbed at floating planks and prayed and listened for the calls of their fellows, but they were alone on the broad ocean, sick from swallowed salt water and the violent heaving of the sea.

After interminable hours, a ship towered before them in the gloom-shrouded sea; the waves hurled them against it. To their joy, they saw lines trailing in the water around them—flung from the ship for their rescue, they assumed. They clutched at the ropes with cold-stiffened fingers and cried out to be pulled up onto the deck, but no answer came. Finally, with strength born of desperation, the two men scaled the vessel's flank, fell over the rail onto the deck, and lay there, panting.

She was an old ship, bulky and broad-beamed. The forecastle and poop loomed black against the sky, blotting out emerging stars. But the men hardly noticed that the rain had stopped, that the winds had subsided and that

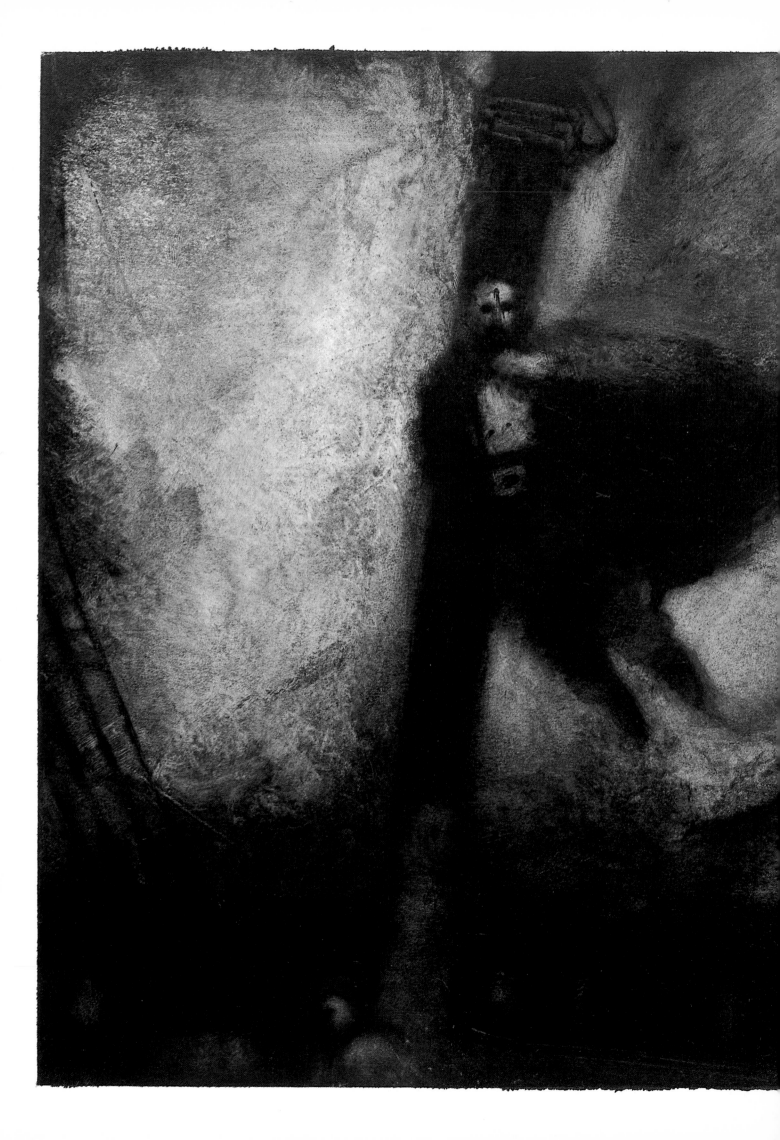

the sky was clearing. They were caught at once in the nightmare on the deck.

Bodies lay everywhere, bodies with open, speechless mouths and eyes that stared vacantly upward; bodies with blackened wounds where knife or cutlass had torn flesh and sinew. They lay among their weapons. Above them on the mainmast, the figure of a man swung with the roll of the ship. A foot-long spike, driven through the skull, fixed the sagging corpse to the spar. The man wore a captain's cloak.

After observing this horrifying tableau for some moments, the merchant stooped and tried to shift one of the dead men from his place. The body lay as if frozen to the deck; no amount of effort would move it. The Spaniard crossed himself then, and gestured to his servant, and the pair picked their way through the carnage to shelter belowdecks. Through cabins and passageways they walked, their footsteps echoing. Nothing was alive here, not even a scuttling rat. They found only old ship's biscuit and water barrels, clothes of antique fashion, a quadrant and some yellowing charts.

After a while, the silence and stale air grew too oppressive to bear. The two men dressed themselves in dry clothing and climbed topside again. The wind was calm; the heavens, washed by the storm, were crystalline. Sighting on the polestar and Orion, the merchant set the ship on a northeast course to Spain and lashed the wheel in place. Immediately afterward, exhausted, he and his servant dropped to the deck and fell asleep among the dead men.

Their rest was troubled. They dreamed that the dead arose, that the captain's cloak flapped past them and that his heavy boots shook the planks. When they awoke, however, the deck was the same, a field of mortality, and the captain still swung on his gibbet. But the night had wrought a change: The shadow of the mainmast was cast forward toward the bow, and the lashings were gone from the wheel. Something had freed the ship and altered its direction: It was heading west. The merchant again set it on course toward Spain. He and his servant stood at the wheel all that long day, two living creatures among the

motionless dead. When night fell, they lashed the helm and went below; the cabins at least were empty of corpses.

After lighting an oil lamp to keep away the dark, they retreated to a corner of the main cabin and sank into sleep. A shout, hanging in the air as from a dream, woke them. The lamp suspended from the ceiling swung wildly, casting pools of light that spread and vanished, showing scenes in flashes: seamen shouting curses from twisted faces, the captain braced behind an overturned table, then the captain again, swinging a cutlass that caught a sailor in the throat, then an arcing gout of blood. The lamp went flying, and darkness gripped the cabin. Footsteps hammered on the deck. Above them the fight continued: Swords rang, men screamed.

Silence fell at last, and in the stillness, the two men heard the groan of straining wood and rigging. A rope snapped, sharp as a whipcrack, and the ship heeled. Once more, she was changing course. The Spaniards waited for daylight before venturing from their refuge. The morning was clear; on deck, the dead men lay unmoving as before, and the captain on the mast swayed gently in the dawn breeze. The ship was bearing west.

The servant regarded the corpses with compassion. He was an old man, reared among shepherds in the remote reaches of the Pyrenees, and ghosts were not strangers to him. "Master," he said, "let us give these poor men rest." The merchant nodded, and his servant, with infinite gentleness, walked among the dead, touching each on forehead and breast and whispering words over them that the merchant did not understand. At his touch, the rigid forms softened into the semblance of sleep. Peace descended on the damned. "I know of one who will set this ship forever at rest," said the servant. Understanding, his master nodded assent.

Again they shaped a course for Spain, and this time a fair wind carried them speedily to the coast. Heading toward the Strait of Gibraltar, they steered south for Tangier and its scholars of old magic, who dwelled beyond the reach of the Spanish Inquisition's fires.

They dropped anchor off Tangier. There,

the servant rowed to shore, climbed onto the quay and disappeared into the twisting white streets of the city.

He returned late in the day, bringing with him another old man, whose face was hidden in the depths of his scholar's hood. The elder surveyed the ship and the dead men and said, "These seafarers are restless because they have been cursed for evil action. Dust will free them." And from the folds of his robe he drew a handful of soil, scattering grains carefully over the forehead of each corpse. As he did so, the body wavered and crumbled to dust, leaving not so much as a belt or button behind.

He turned to the captain last—and a wonder happened. When the grains of earth touched the pinioned head, blood welled from the terrible wound. At the same time, flecks of color returned to the sun-darkened cheeks, and the bony hands shuddered to life. The dark mouth opened, and a reedy, aged voice told the ship's tale. It spoke of a passenger whom the crew had cast overboard long years before, greedy for the gold he carried; it told of how he had cursed the seamen as he died, calling down bitter battling among them, and deaths to be suffered again and again, until such time as the crew once more touched earth. It told how the curse had come true, how the men had mutinied, how the captain had slaughtered them, how two surviving seamen had nailed the master to his own mainmast before they collapsed beneath his dangling boots.

And with that final word, the captain's cracked voice ebbed away. While the three living men gazed, he himself slowly faded: His buckled shoes dissolved, and the bare mast showed through his worn leggings. Cape, shirt and neck all fluttered and grew dim, until nothing was left but the bearded head pinned by a spike to the mast. At the last, the tormented head, too, disappeared from sight. The deck was empty, save for the merchant and his servant, who understood cursing, and the scholar of Tangier, who knew old magics that would break old spells. The ship was free now, to answer to living hands and sail in the healthy light of day.

Chapter Four

Perilous Borderlands

On the Bithnian coast by the Sea of Propontis, harvesting and hay-making began in late spring, when the sparkling Pleiades rose and set with the sun and myriad spirits of earth and water were released from the quiescence of winter. From their places of concealment, these elder beings observed the world's seeming masters—alien human folk who went about their petty business and never noticed the creatures hidden in tree and field and spring and stream. Sometimes, for reasons no mortal could fathom, the old ones reached out to men and women. Their touch brought both delight and sorrow, as the Greeks of Bithnia knew well. The people of that land spoke often of the fate of a youth called Bormus, so perfectly handsome that he was known as the darling of the gods. Here is his tale:

One April day, like others of his clan—his father and brothers, the companions of his father's house, the landless helots who served them—Bormus was in the fields lending his strength to the gathering-in of wheat and barley and the cutting of the hay. The valley in which the grainfields lay was long and golden, flanked by hills silver in their mantle of olive trees and brown where the young grape vines climbed the slopes. In the cloudless dome of the sky, the sun blazed with dry, baking power. Young Bormus strode beside his brothers, swinging his scythe through the grain in smooth, sweeping strokes and singing as he worked. Behind the men, small boys chattered and skylarked as they gathered great armfuls of the shorn grain to be bound and stored in ricks for drying. Higher and higher the sun rode, whitening as it approached its apogee and burning on the young men's shoulders and sweat-slicked backs. Toward noon they paused, wiping their faces and squinting across the fields toward the hillsides with their patches of green shade. "Give us a pull at the water jug," said one of Bormus' brothers.

He reached for an earthenware vessel that was lying among scattered wheatstalks. It was empty, as were the jugs that lay beside it. "Gods," he said. "Where is a boy to fetch a drink?"

But Bormus had seen the children flop down in the shade of uncut grain as soon as the men stopped cutting. He was a kindly fellow, and not many years before, he had been a boy himself, gathering the stalks with aching, scratched arms. So he said, "I'll go," and set off with the jugs swinging easily from his strong hands. At the edge of the field, he released an ass from the tree where it was tethered and strapped the water jugs to its back. He gave the beast a slap on the flank to set it going; then he strode beside it up the dirt path that led into the hillside olive groves. Soon the ass stepped more briskly. It sensed that cold water was near.

And so it was, on a low ridge where the sea could be seen gleaming in the distance. Amid a stand of aged trees was a pool, formed centuries before by rimming a fresh-water spring with rock.

Bormus let the ass drink; then he took the water jugs, allowing the beast to wander away and crop the grass. But he did not fill the jugs at once. This was a place and a moment to be savored. He sat on the edge of the pool, enjoying the cool air that hovered over the water and listening to the cicadas celebrate the bright noon. The notes of goatherds' pipes floated down from pastures higher on the hillside. From the fields far below came the cheerful shouts of the harvesters Bormus had left behind. Beside him on a patch of sun-warmed rock, a lizard basked.

Then the water lilies trembled in the quiet pool. The water rippled and whispered against the stones. The lizard scampered out of sight. Bormus stared into the water, caught in the spell of the place.

From among the lilies rose a woman, infinitely seductive, infinitely mysteri-ous. Her skin was whiter than the lily petals; her eyes were leaf green. Dark hair streamed over her glistening shoulders and melted into the water; leaf stems were entwined in the strands. She raised a hand, and Bormus swayed toward her. Then he hesitated and drew back.

"You are not mortal, maiden," he said.

The woman gave a lazy smile and shook her head and beckoned, and the young man's eyes darkened with desire. He bent over the pool.

The instant his fingertips touched the water, the woman seized his wrist with a grip of iron. Sharp little nails dug into his flesh, and the slender arm drew Bormus inexorably down into the water, down into the airless world beneath the earth, where water spirits still reigned and humans could not live.

Or so Bormus' companions later said. The ass had trotted down into the fields unled, giving a doleful bray. Then they climbed to the pool and found the water jugs lying empty and the shadows gathering in the evening chill. They searched and called, but without hope: Something of old magic lingered in the air around the pool. Later, after they had given up the search, the Bithnians made a song for Bormus, saying how he was taken by the nymph of a pool. They sang it for centuries, to the wail of mourning flutes, each year as they wound through the fields to the grain harvest.

In those days of kingdoms and colonies, of fortress cities rearing proud stone walls on promontories, of fields that stretched as far as the eye could see, humankind felt secure in the world. The edges of their territory were not safe, however: The land was girdled by vast oceans, and the earth was laced with subterranean waters. At the borderlines between land and water — the beaches that rimmed the oceans, the reed-fringed shores of lakes, the banks of brooks and rivers — men and women sometimes encountered the ancient beings of the aquatic realm. Such meetings were filled with hazard for mortals. Although they were wonderfully alluring, water people were of a nature little like that of humanity. Incomprehensible magic flowed in their veins.

Even the natural laws of their world were different and spelled danger, as those humans knew who had answered their calls and crossed the boundaries of their territories. The Japanese, for instance, often told the tale of one such adventurer, a man named Urashima, who paid a high price for rending the veil that hung as a barrier between the worlds of land and sea.

Urashima lived in the province of Tango in southern Honshu, by the shores of Ise Bay. He was no more distinguished than the other men of his village, which was a small one of thatch-roofed wooden houses and narrow dirt streets, but he was a good man.

One gray autumn day, when the houses were shuttered against the chill winds that blew off the bay and the fishermen's shallow boats were beached in net-draped rows in the sand, Urashima walked alone along the shore and found an ugly little scene. A sea turtle, aged, trailing seaweed, had been washed in with the tide. It lay helpless on the ground, scraping awkwardly at the sand with its flippers. Some small

When they chose to take human form, the spirits of wells and pools were infinitely enticing to mortals, but their sweet embrace was a route to ruin.

boys of the town were tormenting it. They did not dare approach the beast too close, but they circled around their victim, pelting it with stones and squealing with laughter. As soon as they saw Urashima, they dropped their rocks on the sand, and at a jerk of his head, they dispersed. Urashima let them go. With a sigh, he turned toward the turtle. Crouching and straining, he shoved it across the beach toward the water, so that it might swim to freedom. Progress was slow. The turtle groaned but it did not snap at him, and at last he moved it to a point where the waves lapped at its shell.

Urashima stepped back to let the sea beast take to the water, but the turtle remained where it was. Slowly, it raised its warted head, looking at him from hooded eyes. Then a guttural voice issued from the beaklike mouth.

"Fisherman," said the turtle, "the sea's thanks for your goodness. Let the sea reward you; I will carry you to the place of the lord who rules these waters."

The fisherman hesitated a moment. He looked back at the familiar roofs of the town, half-hidden in a haze of pungent wood smoke; at the path that ran along the boat-strewn beach, where chickens pecked in the dirt and pigs rooted. He looked at the sea, spread clean and broad and iron gray, with flecks of white where the wind slapped at the waves. Then he climbed on the turtle's leathery back and curled his fingers around the edge of the thick shell. The wrinkled neck stretched, and the beast heaved itself forward.

With powerful strokes of its flippers, the turtle rowed the waves; awkward no more, it flew through its element, a bird in the water. Salt spray spattered Urashima's face, and he laughed with the delight of it. He laughed even when the turtle dived and the sea closed over his head.

He did not drown; his eyes did not darken, nor his lungs fill, for magic shielded him and let him live in the alien element. Down into the depths the turtle swam in lazy circles, descending through forests of seaweed. From the shadows, the bright eyes of innumerable creatures watched their passage. Then turtle and rider cleared the waving fronds. Beneath the sea forest, a countryside spread out, a place with coral woods and rolling hills where boys shepherded schools of fish. Small farms lay in the valleys. Rising in the center of this country was a palace, tier upon tier of scarlet pavilions crowned with tiles of gold and ornamented with gilded dragons. Here the turtle alighted, and Urashima slid to the ocean floor.

He was in the sea lord's garden. Tall trees that he did not recognize surrounded it, swaying in a gentle underwater wind. The flowers gave forth light, and among the flowers a woman waited. She had the slenderness, the pale skin and the almond eyes of a great court lady. Her outer kimono was of brocade as green as the sea, and swags of pearls adorned the long combs that held up her hair. Urashima prostrated himself. All his life he had heard tales of the sea king's daughter.

But the lady took his hands in hers, raised him to his feet and led him to a teahouse. There, it was said, he feasted for three days, served by fish slaves and caressed by the daughter of the sea lord. As if he had been a lord himself, Urashima lay at his ease in the underwater world.

But it was a world in constant motion. Everything in it—the fish, the trees, the palace, the lady herself—shimmered and shifted in ceaseless currents. Urashima was an earthling; he came to long for the comforting solidity of the land.

When he begged to return to his own world, the lady regarded him somberly for a moment. Then she nodded. She embraced him and put into his hands a small lacquered box tied with silk, such as court women used to hold their jewels.

"Keep this always by you, and I will serve as your guardian on the land," she said. "Do not open it, for then its power will fade into sea mist and water."

Above them, a shadow moved; the turtle approached and bowed its ancient head to the man. Urashima mounted as before, and the turtle carried him up above the sea palace, above the wooded hills, through the seaweed forests and into the realm of air. It left him on the shore and swam away without a backward glance.

The man stood on the beach, clutching his lacquer box and gazing in bafflement at what he saw. The outlines of the village had changed. Tile roofs shone among the thatched ones, and the plum blossoms of spring nodded behind garden walls. The beach was bare of boats.

He wandered through strange stone streets, making his way toward the edge of the village, where his own cottage had stood. There he found bare earth. Lying on the ground was a stone washbasin that he recognized, but that was all. Urashima buried his head in his hands and wept.

A voice spoke, and he turned to see an old man observing him with curiosity. "Tell me the fate of the family of Urashima," he said to the old man.

The man raised his brows. His face creased into a thousand wrinkles, and he said, "Why, we have heard of them, from our grandfathers' grandfathers. This was their land, where you stand now. The old men say that the last of them died three hundred years ago. He went into the sea, they say, and never returned." He gave Urashima a thoughtful pat on the shoulder and shuffled off.

So Urashima stood alone, a ghost, it seemed, in his own world, trapped by the magic of the waters, where a day spanned a hundred years of earthlings' time. He turned the lacquer box slowly in his hands: No reason now not to open it and find what treasure there might be. He untied the ribbon that bound the lid.

Accounts differ as to the contents of the box. Some said it contained a feather, a cloud of white smoke and a mirror. Some said that only sea mist rose from it, shaped into the face of the sea king's daughter, and that this mist swept past Urashima and floated out across the sea, whispering mournfully.

All agreed, however, that when the magic of the lacquer box was freed, Urashima's life as a man was over. His face sagged, his body stooped, and he seemed to dissolve. According to some tales, he sank to the ground and vanished into

Through the grace of water magic, the
    fisherman Urashima feasted with a sea lord's
daughter in a teahouse on the ocean floor.

The fisherman Urashima left the palace of the sea lord to return to his own
village; a giant turtle was his steed. But he found that his home was home no more.

dust. According to others, the feather clung to him, the mist enveloped him, and in the mirror he saw his young man's face grow wrinkled and old and the bones break through the skin. In the next instant, a white crane stood on stilt legs in the place where Urashima had been. He had been transformed, it was said, into the bird of longevity because of his centuries under the sea. The people said that sometimes the crane would stalk the beach beside the town, and a great sea turtle would quietly emerge from the water to see it. In memory of the pair, the people at the great shrine at Ise made a dance that they called "Crane and Turtle."

In days gone by, people knew that shore creatures, such as the turtle, partook of the shore's shifting and perilous character. Although they wore the form of animals that breathed air and maintained some attachment to land, they were sons and daughters of the waves, and their presence was invariably a threat to mortals. Sometimes such beasts served simply as bearers of bad tidings. In centuries past, British fishermen believed that when curlews flew up and down the shore crying persistently, the birds were warning of shipwreck and death for those who ventured out. In the north of France, cormorants that hunched on coastal rocks, drying their angled wings, were thought to be waiting for fishermen's souls. And all along the coasts of Europe, shorefolk regarded gulls with awe. Circling high overhead, the birds served as a benison for shipbuilders, but Breton sailors believed that harsh cries from gulls before a launch portended death at sea.

Gulls were said to clothe the souls of drowned sailors. Shetland Islanders, for instance, were fond of telling of a coastal wrecker who found the corpse of a seaman washed ashore one night. He stripped it of clothes, boots and belt; he even took the sailor's lucky golden earring, and he left the naked body to roll aimlessly back and forth in the waves, trapped between land and sea by rocks. From that time, the wrecker was a haunted man. Night after night, a gull beat against the windowpanes of his cottage, seeking entry and shrieking savagely, until at last the man went mad: The soul of the dead sailor had exacted its revenge. So strong was the belief in the human souls of gulls that fishermen called it an act of charity to feed them and a crime to kill them.

Some shore creatures were more than harbingers or embodied ghosts. Like the shore, they were a species unto themselves, partaking of both land and sea. Among such beings were the selkies of northern coasts – of Scotland, Ireland and Iceland. By day the selkies assumed the form of the gray seals that basked on the shore rocks and fished the shallow waters, slow and lumbering on land, sleek and swift among the waves. By night they walked as men and women.

Who and what were they? In the Shetland Islands they were said to be members of the Fin Folk, a race of tribes that gardened the sea bottom just offshore – hidden lands where the seaweed grew in every color of the rainbow, where crystal palaces stood, lit by twinkling phosphorus and gilded with the shifting sheen of the northern lights. In the Orkney Islands and along the Scandinavian coasts, however, the selkies were said to be the form that drowned men and women took after death.

All agreed, however, that at certain times – some said every ninth night, some said only once a year on Midsummer Eve – a mortal man or woman brave enough to walk lanternless on the shore would see a lovely sight. The moon would rise, and in the path of light it made across the water, dark heads would gleam – seals, swimming to the shore. They would flop onto the silvered shore rocks; for some moments they would rest, seal fashion, with their chins on the stone. Then the beasts would tremble and rise, and their pelts would slide in silky folds to the ground. The animals were no longer seals but the fairest of maidens; their cries were not the harsh barks and coughs of seals but the sweetest of women's songs. Singing, they would dance in the moonlight until the stars began to set. Then they would stoop and slide into their sealskins. Maidens no more, they would flop back into the sea and vanish.

Island men said that he who could steal one of the pelts while the maidens danced could have a maiden for his own, for without her sealskin, she could not return to the waves. As long as their sealskins were kept hidden away, such women made pretty and faithful wives, although they mourned for their watery homes. Some mortal men even fathered children with their sea wives. In time, however, the women always found their transforming sealskins and returned to the sea, leaving their earthbound husbands bereft and their human children orphaned. No union could be permanent between the races of the waters and those of the land.

Still, the children of such loves – boys and girls whose fingers and toes were delicately webbed – were not uncommon in the northern islands of Scotland, where the sea's presence was always close. Nor were they feared; people thought of the children as a special grace from the sea, bearing an enchantment.

Sometimes such children were fathered by selkies. Island people told of women who summoned selkie lovers. A maiden had only to go alone to the shore and shed seven tears into the water to call forth a selkie. When the salt tears struck the salt sea, a man would rise from the waters, casting off a sealskin as he appeared. He would lie with the woman there on the shore, and then he would vanish. Later she would bear his child. Some of these children stayed with their mothers; some, however, were reclaimed by their fathers when they were young. In either case, their lives were restless. Being creatures of both earth and ocean, they were always torn, always feeling the pull of one or the other element.

No such poignance attended the mermaids – beautiful women with fish tails instead of legs. These shore haunters were thought in Scotland to be part of the Fin Folk, like the selkies. But mermaids ranged far from northern shores, and they were far older than the selkie tribe. According to ancient tales, they were daughters of Aphrodite, the foam-born goddess of love, whose companion was the dolphin, king of fishes. In token of this ancestry, mermaids carried Aphrodite's ornaments: mirrors emblematic of the glowing planet Venus, and ivory combs, which signified the goddess's powerful femininity.

Seductive, celestial singers, mermaids were a threat to men: They lured humans into the watery realm and trapped their souls there. The love of a mermaid always meant death in the end — a death without the burial that would give the soul peace. So alluring were these creatures that images of them — complete with mirror and comb — were carved in churches from Bologna to Yorkshire as warnings against the sensual vices. And so frightening were they in their beauty that the sight of a mermaid on the shore, combing her long locks and singing her sea song, was said to be a portent of terrible storms.

The seashore was not the only borderland between water and earth, of course. The counterparts of mermaids, selkies and other beings of the sea's verge lived along the margins of the inland waters, as well. Descendants, perhaps, of old forgotten gods, these solitary spirits lurked among the reeds that fringed rivers, or hid in the depths of quiet ponds, or laired behind the drapery of waterfalls, waiting for unwary human victims.

Fluidity of shape was a characteristic of many of them, and they could present the most appealing of appearances. The shoopiltie of Shetland pools, for instance, generally was seen as a small pony capering beside still water, but it sometimes adopted the form of a young man. It lured folk to the water's edge and overpowered

them: The food that sustained it was the blood of the drowned. Similarly, the *necks* of Scandinavia might manifest themselves as boats or small dogs, or green-eyed old men with dripping beards, or simply as hollow voices echoing across the waters, demanding the sacrifice of a life each year.

Some of the inland water dwellers were hideous grotesqueries. The *kappa*, or *kawako* (child of the river), of Japan — a goblin that fed on human livers — was a twisted, monkey-like brute with horny skin and webbed fingers; the *kappa* had a shallow depression on the top of its skull, filled with the river water that gave it life. And hovering in the current of the River Tees in the north of England was a green-haired, slack-jawed, green-toothed hag named Peg Powler. She was a huntress, and the tender flesh of small children was her favorite fare.

A number of these creatures — among them, the nymph that tempted Bormus to his doom — were as lovely as any mermaid. They were water guardians, it was true, but they were also skilled in enchantment, and it was their will to separate their victims from the human community and make them the servitors of elder powers.

In Scotland once, such a one haunted a quiet pool, sometimes in the shape of a pretty brown trout, and sometimes in the form of a maiden as graceful as the birches that swayed beside the water. Although no one could tell how it happened, she seduced a young man named Colvill; he took to leaving his fellows to attend her at her pool. All one summer, he would lie

In Scotland, it was said that maidens sometimes summoned selkie lovers to
the shore by weeping into the water. The selkies walked on land as men, and gave the
women children. Then they vanished into the sea as seals, leaving the mothers bereft.

among the trees in the nymph's arms.

He might have wasted his life in this manner, had not his family arranged a marriage for him with a mortal woman as blithe and gay as summer itself. Colvill stayed by her side for some days after the wedding, apparently charmed away from the dangers of the other world. But his wife unwittingly sent Colvill back to his water maiden. She had heard of his trysts. One afternoon, in the garden of his father's house, she prettily begged him not to visit the pool again.

Colvill stood in the groomed garden and stared at his lady, at her gleaming braids in their tight coils, at her stiff brocaded gown, bound at the waist by a heavy golden belt that he had given her for her bride's gift. And in the midst of this decorum, an image came to him of the mountain pool with its delicate birches, of the water nymph's tossing hair and of her leaf brown, laughing eyes. Colvill turned and left his wife where she stood.

In her upland home, at ease in the flickering shadows that the birches cast on the grass, the water nymph awaited him, almost invisible among the leaves, trailing long fingers in her pool. Colvill knelt beside her. She brushed a palm across his hair and said, "And how do you like your new lady?" He shook his head and pulled her into his arms, but the water nymph only smiled at him, a smile as cool as the waters that she guarded.

"Does not your head hurt, then, young Colvill?" she said softly.

Pain stabbed at his temples, so hot and sudden that tears sprang to his eyes.

"Cut a piece of my shift and bind your head; the magic in it will ease the pain."

Colvill did that; with his knife, he cut a strip of the smock that she wore, while the nymph watched him with expressionless eyes. The smile still played on her lips while he bound the silk around his head.

Like a rope of iron, like a torturer's knot, the silky stuff clasped Colvill's skull, tighter and tighter, until the bone cracked and blood poured from his ears. Inside his head he was screaming, but Colvill made no outward sound. He staggered to his feet, clawing at the nymph's bandage. It only tightened under his hand. He turned on her then, drawing a knife, but she whirled out of reach, light as drops of water. She poised for an instant on the edge of her pool. "It is an ill-done thing, young Colvill, to leave me for a mortal maid."

He sank to the ground in a wilderness of pain, and the nymph dived into her pool. When Colvill's people came for him at last, they found him dying. Nothing was to be seen in the pool, save the quick flicker of a brown trout's tail.

The water nymph, having been denied a life, had nevertheless kept that life for her own. It was often so, yet not all water spirits seized their prey from rapacity or for reasons of revenge. There seemed to be a current of attraction that ran between the water people and the people of the earth, a wayward, shifting current, always dammed in the end, for the old ones of the lakes and springs belonged no more in the mortals' world than the mortals did in theirs: Whoever would cross the borders

With a shriek of triumphant laughter and a flash of scales, a water nymph dived
out of the reach of young Colvill of Scotland, the man she would murder with magic.

must leave the lives that they had known.

In Switzerland, for instance, people often told tales of nixes, fairy women of the lakes and streams, who sometimes slipped across the banks and walked among men and women, indistinguishable from the earth dwellers except for the water always falling from the hems of their petticoats.

The Swiss said that the Lake of Zug, cradled in high mountains not far from Lucerne, once harbored a kingdom of nixes, ruled by an Elf King from a palace of glass sunk deep into the lake floor. At night, this Elf King's daughters sometimes

Only the foolhardy lay down to rest near the banks of brooks and the
borders of springs. Solitary nymphs guarded the waters, and the sleeper
might awaken to the sight of beauty that would lure him to his doom.

went among the young men of the village that bordered the lake. In the light of lanterns hung in the village streets, the water women would dance at harvest festivals, only to vanish again at dawn, leaving a trail of waterdrops that led to the edge of the lake.

The parting was not always easy, however. One young nix grew deeply attached to a certain youth of the town, a tall farmer who was quiet and sweet-natured. He, in turn, was charmed by the nix, whose voice was as gentle as the lake waves on the shore and whose hair sparkled with the

Battling a fountain's deadly guardian

Not all spirits of the world's fresh waters took human shape: Near Lerna, on the eastern coast of Greece, laired the Hydra, a beast with a multitude of serpentine heads – one of them immortal – and a breath so venomous that it could kill the living. Its haunt was the fathomless Lernean swamp, where a monstrous crab kept it company. But the Hydra also ranged the fertile district around the marsh, terrorizing all who dwelled there.

The hero Hercules challenged the Hydra once, in the course of his adventures. With his charioteer beside him, he forced the water monster from its lair by pelting it with burning arrows. Enraged, it rushed at him and coiled around his legs, its heads writhing as it sought for a strike. At his feet, its companion crab plucked with enormous pincers.

Hercules crushed the crab with his foot. With his club, he battered the Hydra's heads, and his charioteer seared the stumps with burning brands, for new heads grew when the beast's blood spurted. Then Hercules severed the head that was immortal and buried it deep, muffling the hissing that never stopped. He dipped his arrows in the gall from the body of the Hydra; from that time forward, the hero's arrows, envenomed by the water monster, never failed to kill.

diamonds of a thousand water droplets.

The nix could not stay on land for any length of time and live, however. Eventually, after weeks of nightly meetings, she persuaded her human lover to join her in her lake-bed home. She was skilled in enchantment and cast a spell that let the mortal live under the water, breathing it instead of air, but she could not quell his longing for his own folk, left behind on the land. He pined and wasted in the halls of glass where the nix lived.

Then, said the Swiss, the nix used all her powers to give her lover ease. Between one dusk and dawn, she enspelled his village, summoning it into the depths of the lake. For centuries afterward, those who gazed upon the waters of Zug might see something more than the reflections of snow-capped mountains or parading clouds. If the air was still and the light clear, observers would glimpse an entire town beneath the water—church steeples, steep-roofed houses, winding streets, trees and gardens. And it was no drowned village: People moved there, walking the streets and tending the gardens. When evening fell, lights would wink on in the houses, and then the listener on the shore would hear the church bell sounding the curfew from the depths, calling the nix and her mortal lover to the quiet of their own hearth.

This was a tender tale, much enjoyed by country people: Although estranged from the water and its creatures, such simple folk liked to think that union was yet possible. Most people knew better, especially those who dwelled along the margins of the sea and earned their livelihoods from it. Yet a few mortals who were well aware of the peril posed by water spirits sought them out anyway. One was a Breton youth named Houaru.

Houaru's tale began in a small fishing village named Pont-Aven; it lay at the mouth of the Aven River where that river ran into the sea. The young man had come north from Léon on foot, penniless and without possessions, except for an iron knife and a tiny silver bell. The keepsakes had been given to Houaru by a woman of his own village, who waited for him there while he tried to find a position among the men who fished and worked the Breton oyster beds.

The fisherfolk of Pont-Aven hired him readily enough: He had a strong back and willing hands. But they were insular in that village, suspicious of outsiders. Brittany was rife with dangerous magics then, and no one knew if strangers were what they seemed. They made no effort to draw Houaru in among them.

Still, they saw to it that he had a bed and a place—albeit the stranger's place—in their wineshop when he chose. And it was in the smoky, rushlit shop, on a November night when the rain beat against the shutters and the wind howled outside, that Houaru heard tales of riches from the sea. The men told stories of the isle of Loc'h, and of the gold to be had there for the man who dared to face the treasure's fairy guardian. At last Houaru asked, "Where is this island, then?"

A small silence—a comment on the stranger's curiosity—fell on the room. Finally, one of the fishermen drained his

In the depths of a lake in Switzerland lay an entire, living town, transported there by a water nix so that she could stay forever with her mortal lover.

cup and replied, "At Les Glénans." The man gestured toward the west, and Houaru understood. Les Glénans was a group of rocky islands, usually mist-shrouded, that lay off the Breton coast in the Bay of Biscay. Oyster beds were there, but few men chose to harvest them, for the islands had a sinister reputation, although no one would say why.

Houaru had a taste for adventure, however, and the very next morning he deserted the fisherfolk of Pont-Aven and went searching for treasure. Taking the knife and the bell his sweetheart had given him, he went west to Concarneau, for that fishing town made a good starting point.

At the port, he simply took an unwatched dinghy and sailed the twelve miles out to Les Glénans, where the islands reared their rocky backs from the sullen waters of the bay. Loc'h was easy to find; it was the largest of the group, and trees and flowers shaded its stones. Houaru beached the dinghy in a cove and climbed among the boulders. At his back, mist crept in from the bay, rearing a gray wall around the sunny isle.

Among the trees, he found a still lake bordered by willows. On its shore lay a small boat, painted in scarlet and ornamented with gilt. This was magic indeed: a lake of fresh water on an island surrounded by the sea, and a boat that seemed to beckon even as Houaru looked.

He climbed in without hesitation. Of its own accord, the boat slid from the shore. As the boat moved, it shuddered and softened under him. Houaru found himself straddling warm feathers and riding the back of an enormous swan, as if

he were himself a cygnet. The bird twisted its curving neck to observe him. Then, without warning, while Houaru closed his eyes and clung, it dived.

He opened his eyes only when the rush of water stopped and the swan feathers pulled away from his hands. He stood before a turreted castle, set among gardens and surrounded by forest. This was an enchanted country, swathed in a veil of light. Outside the veil, dark green waters rippled, and high above it, a disk of sunshine showed the surface of the lake. But within the luminous barrier, all was dry and sheltered. At his feet, fish swam in a pond rimmed with black stone.

"Drink this," said a light voice in his ear. A cup of wine was put into his hands. He turned to gaze directly into the eyes of a woman who stood beside him. In that instant, Houaru was lost, drowned in the emerald glance of a nix, a being the Bretons called a *groac'h*. Thoughts of the island treasure he had sought left him. Thoughts of his village and his sweetheart left him. He drank the wine without a word, and the nix chuckled.

"Will you stay with me, young man?" she asked.

He nodded.

"Why, then, we will have a betrothal feast." And the nix stooped, put fish from the pond into a golden basket and turned toward her house. Houaru followed her.

In the hall, a fire blazed, glinting on floors of pale marble and pillars of gold. This was a treasure house, just as the fishermen of Pont-Aven had said. But

Houaru hardly glanced around. He stood with his hands at his sides, quietly waiting for the nix's words.

"It is for you to make the sacrifice," she said, and touched the golden basket. "Give the fish to the fire. Then we will eat them." She left him, and he felt a terrible pang of loss. Nevertheless, he took the basket to the fire. Within it, the fish flopped frantically; a dozen tiny screams echoed in his ear.

And when he touched the first fish with his iron knife, preparing to gut it, it jerked away from his hand and vanished. In its place stood a miniature man, a fisherman like himself.

"Save yourself, fellow," the creature shouted in a reedy voice. "We were all men once." Then the small man dived for cover; iron, proof against enchantment, had freed a human from a nix's spell, although it had not restored him fully, it seemed. Still, Houaru had been saved from murdering one of his own kind. His senses cleared. Horrified, he touched another fish in the basket and then another, and within moments, an army of tiny men swarmed around his feet.

They scattered when a low snarl rolled through the room. The nix had returned; she stood tall and slender, the panels of her long robe foaming around her feet and a silvery net dangling from one hand.

"Do you fear to join my service?" she cried, and Houaru backed away, his knife clattering to the floor.

The last he saw of the nix's face was her green eyes glittering as her net ballooned above his head. Then she seemed suddenly to grow, soaring toward the ceiling in a swirl of silk. The silver bell his sweetheart had given him fell from his shirt, ringing wildly through the hall. A chill descended on his skin. He tried to scream, but only a hoarse croak came from his throat.

"Now, then, little toad," said a voice high above Houaru's head, "it's time you sought the mud, where toads belong." A hard shoe sent him rolling and sliding across the floor. Houaru sprang, and powerful toad's legs carried him beyond the nix's reach. He achieved the door to the hall and hid panting in the grass outside.

How long Houaru was confined in the nix's country, he never afterward could tell, for the light never changed there, and time rolled by flat and golden. He crouched at the edge of the pond, where he could see the captive fish and hear their little voices when they spoke. For the most part, however, the fish kept to the depths, and Houaru shrank among the greenery, out of reach of the nix's grasping hands and trampling feet. Sometimes the nix sang to herself, and high above his head he could hear her croon of power, of earthlings caught in the water's thrall, of sea enchantments, of the victories of the waves.

A day arrived, however, when another victim appeared at the nix's palace. This was a woman, and a young one. Above her black stockings, the many petticoats of the Breton costume flared, and the hem of her dress was embroidered in the pattern of his own village. By her foot rested the tip of a shepherdess's staff.

She spoke to the nix, and her voice was

This was the fate of the men and women whom the waters took away:
        to lie forever unburied in the deep, prey to fish and home to coral,
    gazed upon by the indifferent eyes of drifting water nymphs.

124

calm and low, although Houaru could not distinguish the words. Horrified, he called a warning, but he could only make a toad's guttural croak. With nervous flicks of their shining tails, the fish jackknifed and vanished to the depths of the pond.

In the next moment, the world exploded. Bright wine splashed onto the grass; a silver-colored net blossomed high above. The nix gave a groan like the roaring of the winter sea, and then vanished. Houaru groaned himself, ascending dizzily into the air.

He landed solidly on both feet, and stood trembling, a man once more. The Breton maid gave him a placid smile and called him "sweetheart." She was his own dear maiden from his own village, come to rescue him.

"Brave maid!" he cried. "But how did you find me?"

"You need the old wives' magic against the water magic," she replied. "My silver bell called me; this staff brought me. And cold iron undid the enchantment. The nix is a toad herself now, but she will not long be so. Find your fellows." And together the mortal man and woman searched the pond, touching the enchanted fish one by one with an iron-bladed knife so that they too became men again, defying the power of the place. She told everyone to link hands. Then her staff began to glow and move. It pulled the human chain up through the lake, up into the freedom of the air.

Old wives' wisdom saved the mortal, but it could not forever defeat the power of the water. In after years, Bretons told new tales of the isle of Loc'h, of captives caught in the nix's net of enchantment.

No matter how diminished the stories told about her, no matter how circumscribed her territory, the nix was a child of magnificent magic, heir to the rulers of the world at its dawning, stronger than any land-dwelling race. In her veins flowed the ichor of Oceanus and Tethys, mother of the sea; of cold Ran, devourer of sailors; of mighty Poseidon and of the Nereids; of the Sirens and sea monsters, of mermaids and selkies and all the company of the Fin Folk's underwater empires.

Like them, she was ancient. She was as old as the sea waves that beat against the edges of the land, as old as the springs that bubbled up in mountain forests and swelled into brooks and then streams and finally into profound lakes and the mighty rivers that fed the oceans of the world.

Beautiful and mysterious, life-giving and death-dealing, the waters and the spirits that ruled them had no beginning and no end, no fixity of place or shape, no limits to their power. They were irresistibly attractive to men and women. But mortal men and women were bound to the dust from which they were formed. They could not fly through green depths with the mermaids or sing in the coral caves of the sea. Those who chose water magic were estranged forever from all that made them human, for no door remained open between the worlds. Those caught by the water were doomed to lie forever rooted and silent among the sand and rocks of the depths, frail ghosts swaying in aqueous winds.

A Doomed Alliance of Earth and Water

As capricious as water itself were the beings who made it their home: They seemed to view humans who trod the solid earth with both longing and fear, so that the adventures the two races shared were ringed about with both delight and dread. Tales of such adventures were common once. Among the saddest was that of Huldbrand, lord of the castle of Ringstetten, whose lands lay by the Black Forest, near the source of the Danube.

Huldbrand's story began at a tournament in the city of his Emperor, several days' journey from home. The young knight acquitted himself well in the jousting and the swordplay, and in the festivities that surrounded the tourney, he charmed the court ladies. One of them – a Duke's daughter named Bertalda – was prettier and more daring than the rest. Boldly she dallied with Huldbrand, until he asked for her glove as a token of her favor. She replied that he might have it, if he braved a certain haunted wood near the city and returned to tell her of its wonders. It was a silly maid's whim, but Huldbrand was young and reckless, and it put him on his mettle. Accordingly, one summer morning, he rode alone into the wood.

The place was hardly frightening – at first. The trees were widely spaced, their trunks rosy in the dawn. Beneath the horse's hoofs, the grass grew lush and green; overhead, thrushes and orioles caroled among sun-gilded leaves. But as the day drew in, the trees darkened and loomed, and briars crowded sullenly at their roots. No birds sang, and other sounds – scuttlings and cracklings, mutterings and growls – grew loud. At the edge of vision, sooty creatures crept among the branches, observing Huldbrand

Challenged by a pretty woman, the knight Huldbrand dared the terrors of a haunted wood.

with glittering eyes; strong fingers clutched at his horse's legs, and the animal shivered and showed the whites of its eyes. Frustrated, the knight swung his mount this way and that, seeking the enemy, and thus found himself staring into a face that seemed suspended among the branches. It was an old man's face, white as sea foam, wraithlike in its pallor.

No coward, Huldbrand set his horse straight at this apparition. The instant he moved, however, a torrent of river water replaced the face, roaring toward him with the terrifying force of flood. The horse reared and bolted. Blinded by the stinging spray and herded by the current, the animal plunged into the depths of the wood, bearing Huldbrand with it.

Caught in a maelstrom of wind and water, Huldbrand lost all sense of time; his gallop ended as abruptly as it had begun, and he never could say how long it had taken. His horse stood trembling on the banks of a brook. They had cleared the forest, which stood dark behind them. The brook rushed bubbling over a flowered meadow that formed a peninsula extending into the waters of a placid lake. In the sunlight that slanted across the grass, a cottage stood. At its open door sat an elderly man, lean and weathered, as fishermen were. His nets were spread across his knees and a heavy needle was suspended in his hand; he had stopped his mending to stare at the intruder. The aroma of frying fish drifted from the cottage.

Huldbrand hailed the fisherman, and the old man rose, ducking his head with a countryman's courtesy. The knight asked for pasturage for his horse and shelter for himself, and this was freely given. So when night fell, he found himself in the cottage with the fisherman and the fisherman's wife, his feet warming before a crackling fire and a cup of wine in his hand.

They chatted desultorily, until water rained against the window. The wind was rising. The water splashed again, dribbling through cracks in the window frame, and the fisherman grunted with annoyance. "Leave that, child, and come inside," he called out, and added to Huldbrand, "It is our foster daughter. She is naughty, but there is no harm in her."

At once, the door swung open, and a woman — hardly more than a girl — skipped into the room. Everything about her was bright and glancing. Her pale hair danced and floated around her head, sparkling with waterdrops;

An unsettled creature born of wind and wave, the sea-maiden Undine waited for one to love her.

her eyes were sea green, her skin as pure and luminous as the white crests of waves. She fluttered around the room while the fisherman frowned and his wife clucked with irritation. She alighted near Huldbrand's chair.

"Why, beautiful knight," she said. "Have you been sent to me at last?"

Entranced, Huldbrand put out his hand. The fisherman shook his head, however, and said, "This is no maidenly behavior, Undine." And in her turn the maiden frowned. She rose and stamped her foot; then her anger turned to laughter, and she whirled and ran out of the cottage.

She vanished. But Huldbrand was on his feet, and he followed the maiden into the night. A storm had risen. So dark was the air, so driving the cold rain, so loud the crying of the wind that he quickly lost his way; even the lights of the cottage vanished in clouds of mist. An aged white face shone before him in the gloom; he turned toward it—and slipped into a torrent. Water rose to his waist and tore at his clothes.

"The old man, the prince of the stream, is full of tricks, young knight," a high, clear voice called out. Following it, Huldbrand forced his way through the water and so found Undine, curled in a leafy bower on a little island formed by the flood. He pulled himself up onto the land beside the maiden and took her in his arms to shelter her, and so Huldbrand's heart was lost. They waited out the storm. In the last intervals of the blast, they heard the fisherman's cracked voice calling Undine's name. The willful creature shrugged at the sound, but Huldbrand carried her across the flood to the cottage. A pale face peered at him from the shadows as he went.

After that night, the little promontory was turned into an island and remained so for some days; the brook that ran across it, swelled by the flood, cut it off from the wood that walled it from the world. Huldbrand cared not at all. He stayed at the cottage, hunting waterfowl and fishing and basking in a waking dream that was the love of Undine.

She was mercurial and elusive, bright and loving one instant, cruel and sharp the next. From the man, Huldbrand learned how the couple had found her. Their own infant daughter, it seemed, had vanished some years before, and Undine had appeared at their door several days later. A tiny child, richly dressed and jeweled, she had babbled of crystal palaces under

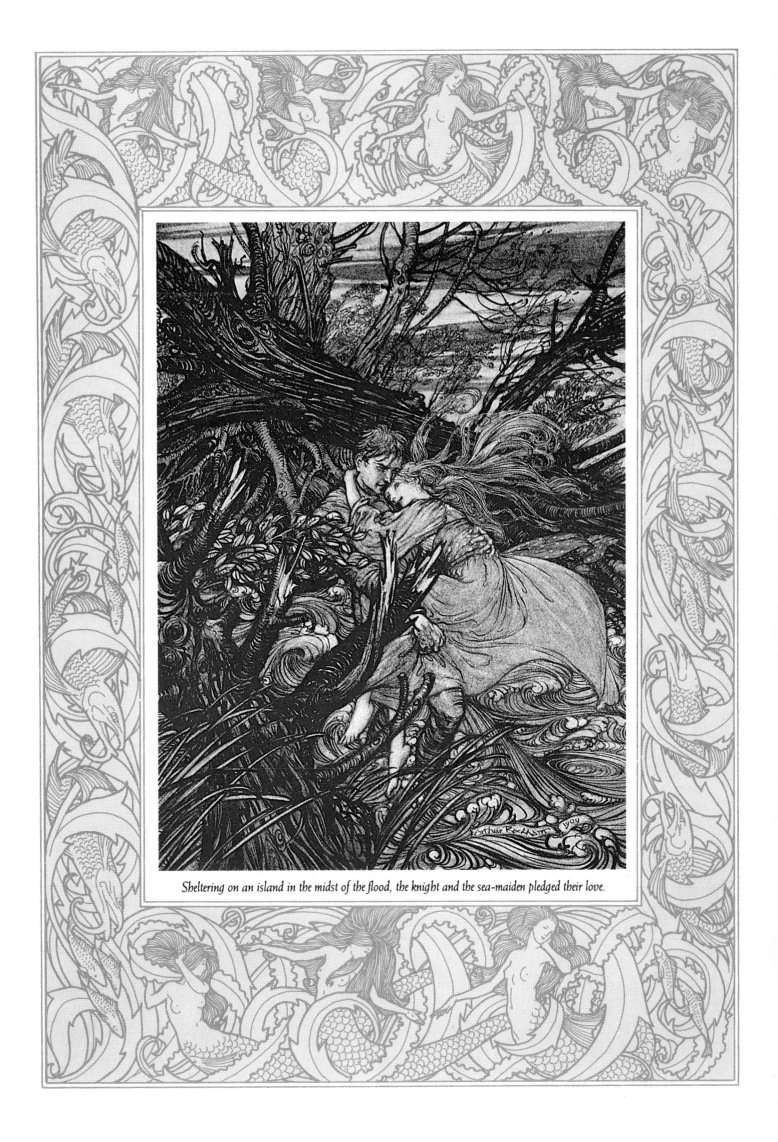

Sheltering on an island in the midst of the flood, the knight and the sea-maiden pledged their love.

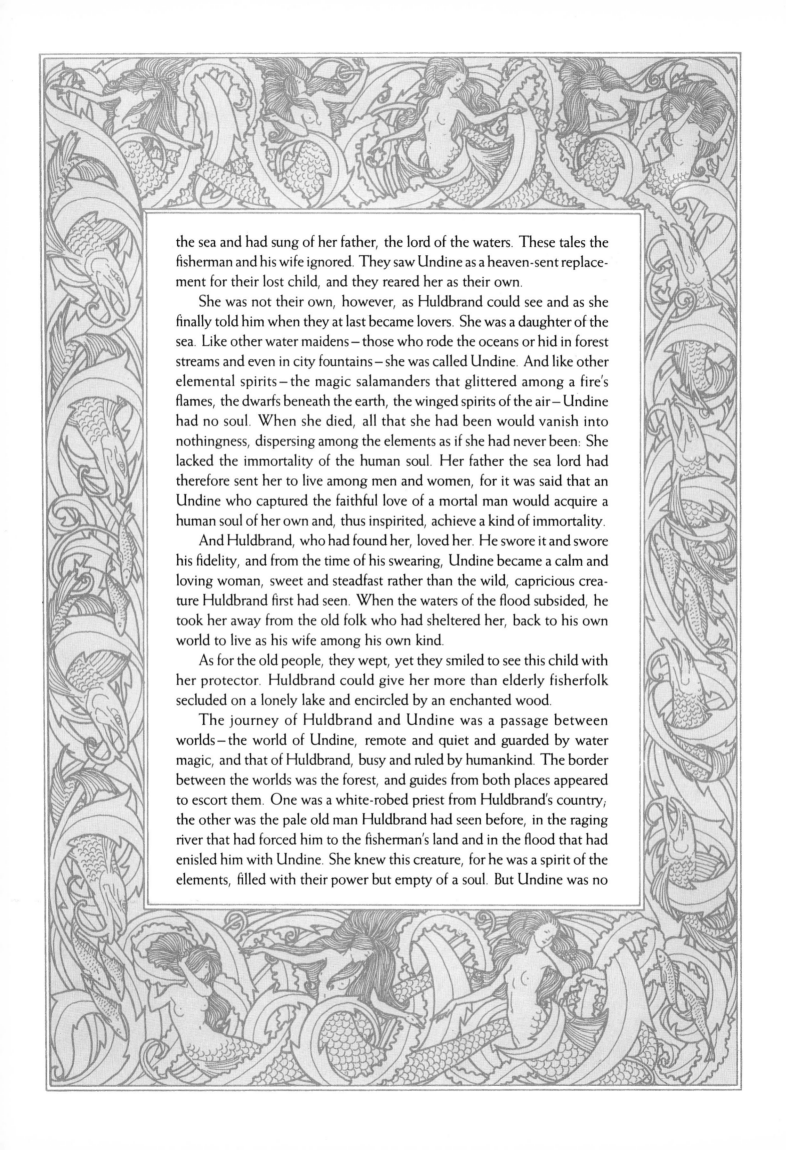

the sea and had sung of her father, the lord of the waters. These tales the fisherman and his wife ignored. They saw Undine as a heaven-sent replacement for their lost child, and they reared her as their own.

She was not their own, however, as Huldbrand could see and as she finally told him when they at last became lovers. She was a daughter of the sea. Like other water maidens – those who rode the oceans or hid in forest streams and even in city fountains – she was called Undine. And like other elemental spirits – the magic salamanders that glittered among a fire's flames, the dwarfs beneath the earth, the winged spirits of the air – Undine had no soul. When she died, all that she had been would vanish into nothingness, dispersing among the elements as if she had never been: She lacked the immortality of the human soul. Her father the sea lord had therefore sent her to live among men and women, for it was said that an Undine who captured the faithful love of a mortal man would acquire a human soul of her own and, thus inspirited, achieve a kind of immortality.

And Huldbrand, who had found her, loved her. He swore it and swore his fidelity, and from the time of his swearing, Undine became a calm and loving woman, sweet and steadfast rather than the wild, capricious creature Huldbrand first had seen. When the waters of the flood subsided, he took her away from the old folk who had sheltered her, back to his own world to live as his wife among his own kind.

As for the old people, they wept, yet they smiled to see this child with her protector. Huldbrand could give her more than elderly fisherfolk secluded on a lonely lake and encircled by an enchanted wood.

The journey of Huldbrand and Undine was a passage between worlds – the world of Undine, remote and quiet and guarded by water magic, and that of Huldbrand, busy and ruled by humankind. The border between the worlds was the forest, and guides from both places appeared to escort them. One was a white-robed priest from Huldbrand's country; the other was the pale old man Huldbrand had seen before, in the raging river that had forced him to the fisherman's land and in the flood that had enisled him with Undine. She knew this creature, for he was a spirit of the elements, filled with their power but empty of a soul. But Undine was no

Undine rode to the world of mortals with two guides: a human priest and a spirit of the waters.

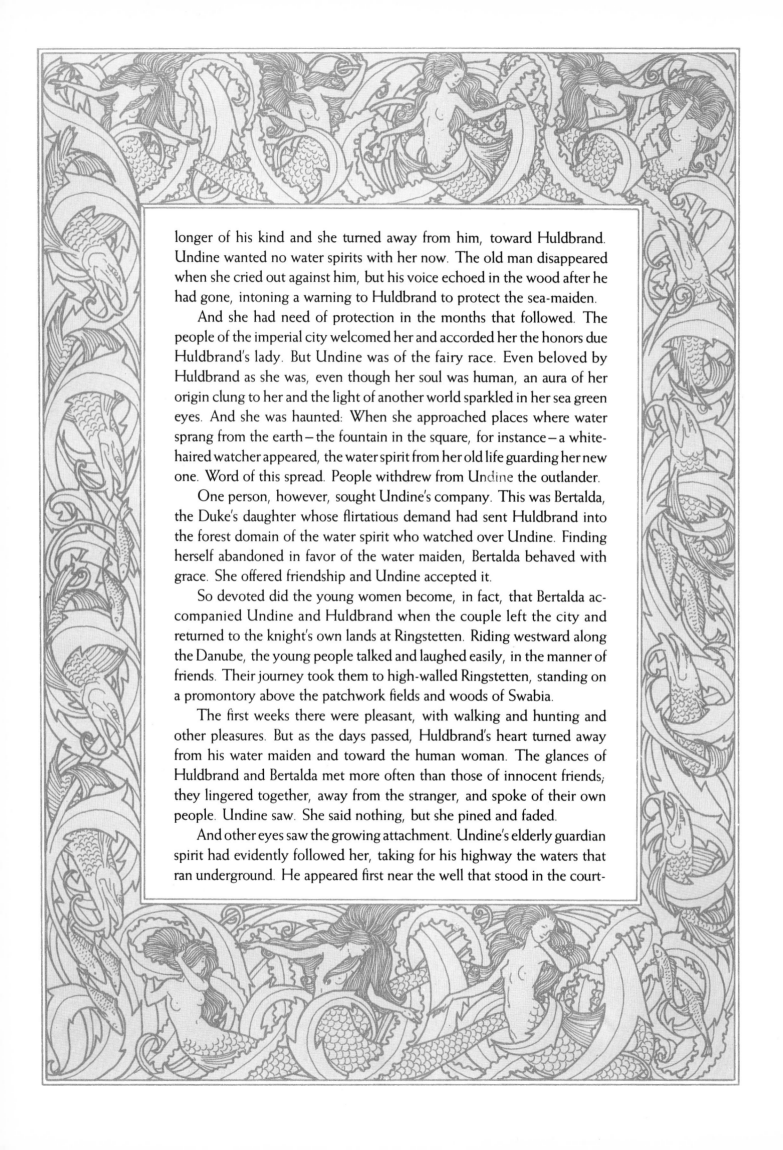

longer of his kind and she turned away from him, toward Huldbrand. Undine wanted no water spirits with her now. The old man disappeared when she cried out against him, but his voice echoed in the wood after he had gone, intoning a warning to Huldbrand to protect the sea-maiden.

And she had need of protection in the months that followed. The people of the imperial city welcomed her and accorded her the honors due Huldbrand's lady. But Undine was of the fairy race. Even beloved by Huldbrand as she was, even though her soul was human, an aura of her origin clung to her and the light of another world sparkled in her sea green eyes. And she was haunted: When she approached places where water sprang from the earth – the fountain in the square, for instance – a white-haired watcher appeared, the water spirit from her old life guarding her new one. Word of this spread. People withdrew from Undine the outlander.

One person, however, sought Undine's company. This was Bertalda, the Duke's daughter whose flirtatious demand had sent Huldbrand into the forest domain of the water spirit who watched over Undine. Finding herself abandoned in favor of the water maiden, Bertalda behaved with grace. She offered friendship and Undine accepted it.

So devoted did the young women become, in fact, that Bertalda accompanied Undine and Huldbrand when the couple left the city and returned to the knight's own lands at Ringstetten. Riding westward along the Danube, the young people talked and laughed easily, in the manner of friends. Their journey took them to high-walled Ringstetten, standing on a promontory above the patchwork fields and woods of Swabia.

The first weeks there were pleasant, with walking and hunting and other pleasures. But as the days passed, Huldbrand's heart turned away from his water maiden and toward the human woman. The glances of Huldbrand and Bertalda met more often than those of innocent friends; they lingered together, away from the stranger, and spoke of their own people. Undine saw. She said nothing, but she pined and faded.

And other eyes saw the growing attachment. Undine's elderly guardian spirit had evidently followed her, taking for his highway the waters that ran underground. He appeared first near the well that stood in the court-

In Huldbrand's world, a rival awaited Undine: the lady Bertalda, who herself desired the knight.

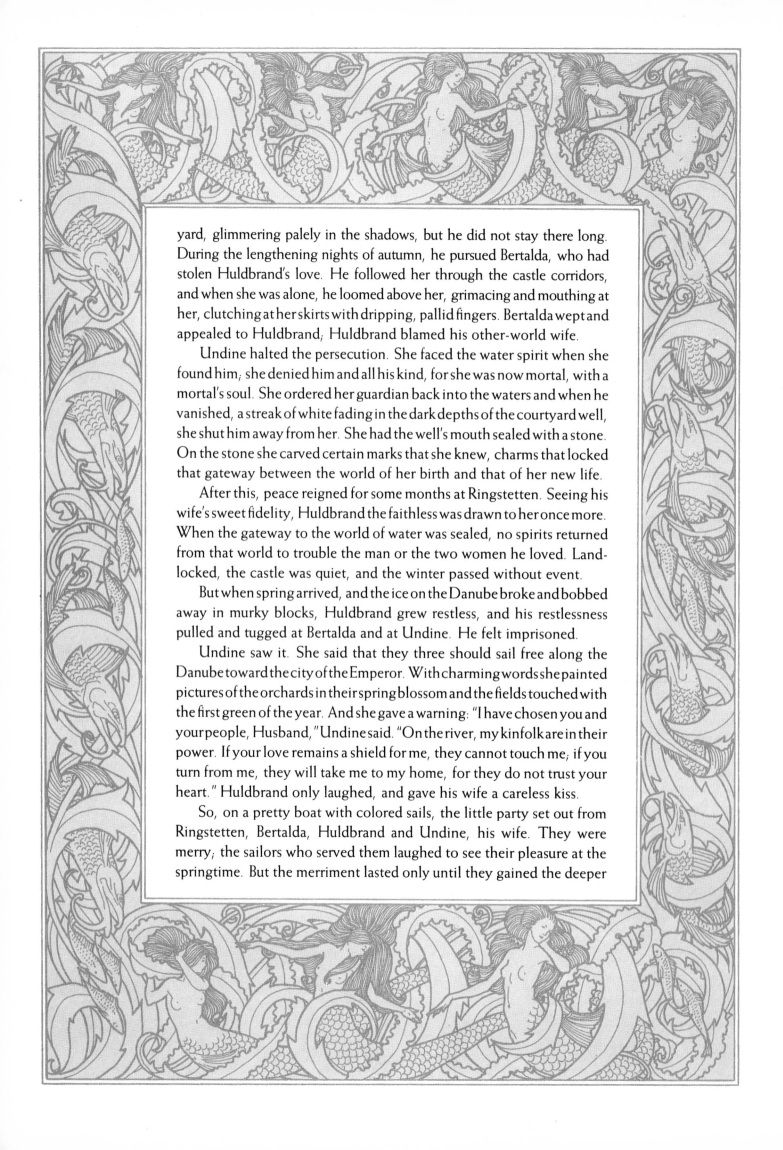

yard, glimmering palely in the shadows, but he did not stay there long. During the lengthening nights of autumn, he pursued Bertalda, who had stolen Huldbrand's love. He followed her through the castle corridors, and when she was alone, he loomed above her, grimacing and mouthing at her, clutching at her skirts with dripping, pallid fingers. Bertalda wept and appealed to Huldbrand; Huldbrand blamed his other-world wife.

Undine halted the persecution. She faced the water spirit when she found him; she denied him and all his kind, for she was now mortal, with a mortal's soul. She ordered her guardian back into the waters and when he vanished, a streak of white fading in the dark depths of the courtyard well, she shut him away from her. She had the well's mouth sealed with a stone. On the stone she carved certain marks that she knew, charms that locked that gateway between the world of her birth and that of her new life.

After this, peace reigned for some months at Ringstetten. Seeing his wife's sweet fidelity, Huldbrand the faithless was drawn to her once more. When the gateway to the world of water was sealed, no spirits returned from that world to trouble the man or the two women he loved. Land-locked, the castle was quiet, and the winter passed without event.

But when spring arrived, and the ice on the Danube broke and bobbed away in murky blocks, Huldbrand grew restless, and his restlessness pulled and tugged at Bertalda and at Undine. He felt imprisoned.

Undine saw it. She said that they three should sail free along the Danube toward the city of the Emperor. With charming words she painted pictures of the orchards in their spring blossom and the fields touched with the first green of the year. And she gave a warning: "I have chosen you and your people, Husband," Undine said. "On the river, my kinfolk are in their power. If your love remains a shield for me, they cannot touch me; if you turn from me, they will take me to my home, for they do not trust your heart." Huldbrand only laughed, and gave his wife a careless kiss.

So, on a pretty boat with colored sails, the little party set out from Ringstetten, Bertalda, Huldbrand and Undine, his wife. They were merry; the sailors who served them laughed to see their pleasure at the springtime. But the merriment lasted only until they gained the deeper

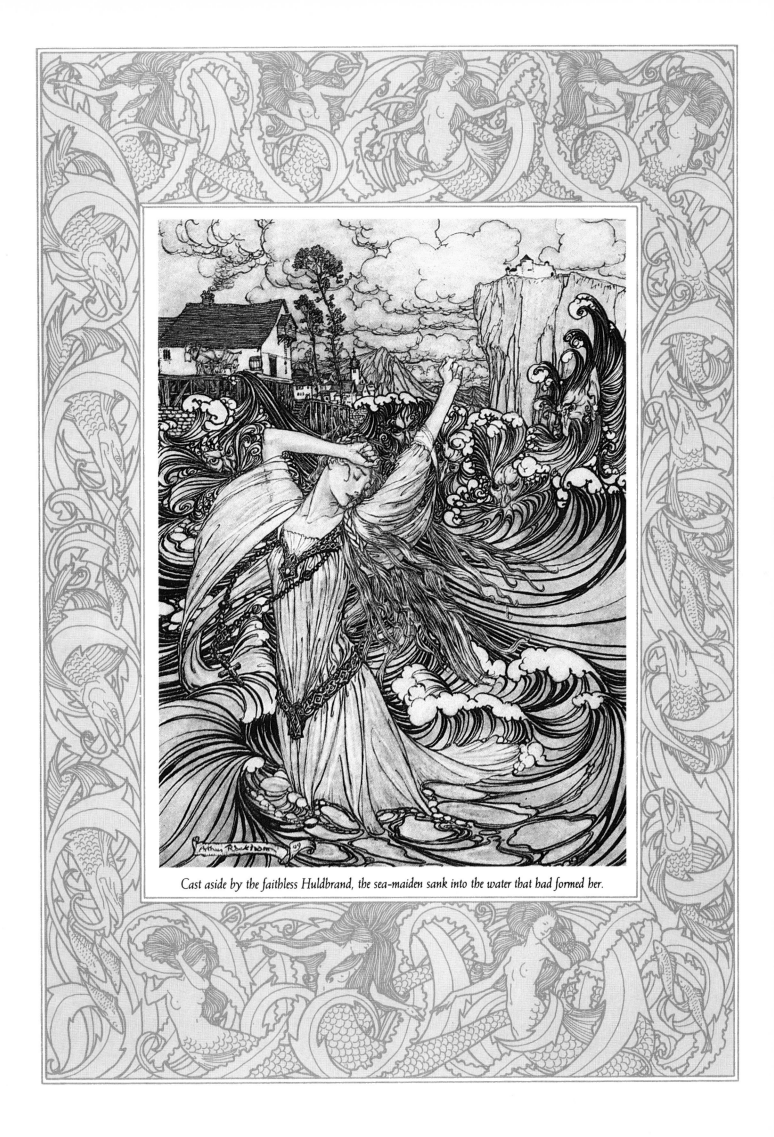

Cast aside by the faithless Huldbrand, the sea-maiden sank into the water that had formed her.

waters at the center of the river. Then the journey became a nightmare.

The waters boiled and foamed around them, and among the whitecaps an ashen head appeared, grinning, disembodied. It squealed meaningless words at Bertalda; she hid her face in her hands; Huldbrand turned on his wife. But Undine gestured pleadingly, and he spoke no unkind word. The moment passed, and the waters calmed. The watery apparition disappeared. Yet the sailors crossed themselves and shook their heads and muttered of sorcery and of people from other worlds.

In a little while, the day was at peace again. Bertalda smiled and trailed her hand in the river, to watch the reflections of a golden chain she held. All saw its glitter – and all saw the death-white fingers that leaped from the water and snatched the chain. Huldbrand's lips tightened. But Undine only smiled; she put her own fingers in the waters and drew out a chain of coral, and this she gave to Bertalda as a consolation for the lost bauble.

"Sorceress," cried Huldbrand then. "You are of the water folk still. You should not walk among humankind." Thus he betrayed his wife.

With no more than a small cry, Undine turned from him. Over the side of the sailboat she slipped, and none could say whether she simply sank or whether she dissolved into the waters. The last that was seen of her was a streak of green and silver in the river's current.

Huldbrand grieved, it is true, but not for long. It was no easy thing to have a wife so strange. He remained at Ringstetten for the mourning period, but Bertalda did too. The day came when he wanted her for his lady. Free from the fear of the other world, his people rolled back the stone that covered the well and prepared to celebrate their master's marriage.

But the power of the waters surrounded him still. It was said that Huldbrand dreamed of Undine, that he saw her weeping in a cave of crystal far beneath the sea and that he groaned to see her. No one knew if the visions were true, but on the day of his wedding, all saw how he walked to the well in his courtyard, eagerly, as if to a lover. All saw the shimmering figure that rose from the well and held out its arms to him. All saw how he vanished for a moment in those arms. He reappeared a dead man, his soul claimed by Undine, the spirit of the sea that he himself had chosen.

In Huldbrand's dreams, Undine shimmered, singing sadly in a crystal palace beneath the sea.

Picture Credits

The sources for the illustrations in this book are shown below. When known, the artist's name precedes the picture source.

Cover: Detail from a painting by J. W. Waterhouse, The Royal Academy of Arts, courtesy The Bridgeman Art Library, London. 1-5: Artwork by Alicia Austin. 6-11: Artwork by John Howe. 15: Artwork by Matt Mahurin. 16, 17: Artwork by John Howe. 18-21: Artwork by Wayne Anderson. 24-27: Artwork by Julek Heller. 28-35: Artwork by Gary Kelley. 36, 37: Artwork by John Howe. 39: W. Russell Flint, from *The Heroes* by Charles Kingsley, © The Medici Society Ltd., 1912, courtesy Mary Evans Picture Library, London. 42, 43: Artwork by John Howe. 46, 47: Walter Crane, courtesy Neue Pinakothek, photographed by Blauel/Gnamm, Artothek, Munich. 50, 51: Herbert Draper, Ferens Art Gallery, Hull, courtesy The Bridgeman Art Library, London. 52-58: Artwork by Julek Heller. 60-67: Artwork by John Howe. 68, 69: Artwork by Matt Mahurin. 72, 73: Artwork by Troy Howell. 74: Courtesy *Ill. Familie Journal*, 1890, Copenhagen. 76-78: Artwork by Matt Mahurin. 80, 81: Kuniyoshi, courtesy B. W. Robinson Collection, photographed by Derek Bayes, London. 84, 85: Artwork by Matt Mahurin. 88, 89: T. J. Dix, courtesy Fine Art Photographic Library Ltd., London. 90: Howard Pyle, courtesy Delaware Art Museum, Howard Pyle Collection. 92-99: Artwork by Matt Mahurin. 100, 101: Artwork by Michael Hague. 103: Edward Burne-Jones, Fogg Art Museum, Harvard University, Grenville L. Winthrop Bequest. 106-108: Artwork by Michael Hague. 112, 113: Artwork by Matt Mahurin. 115: Arthur Rackham, Kunstbibliothek, Berlin, by permission of Barbara Edwards, courtesy Bildarchiv Preussischer Kulturbesitz, West Berlin. 116, 117: J. W. Waterhouse, Roy Miles Fine Paintings, courtesy The Bridgeman Art Library, London. 118: A. F. Gorguet, document *l'Illustration*/Sygma, Paris, courtesy Mary Evans Picture Library, London. 120, 121: Artwork by Troy Howell. 124: Edmund Dulac, copyright Geraldine M. Anderson, from *The Tempest* by William Shakespeare, Hodder and Stoughton, 1908, courtesy Mary Evans Picture Library, London. 126-139: Arthur Rackham, from *Undine* by de La Motte-Foqué, published by William Heinemann, 1909, by permission of Barbara Edwards, courtesy Dorothy Bacon, London. Border artwork adapted from Arthur Rackham by Alicia Austin. 144: Artwork by Alicia Austin.

Bibliography

Anderson, Rasmus B., ed. and transl., *Norse Mythology; or, The Religion of Our Forefathers, Containing All the Myths of the Eddas.* 7th ed. Chicago: Scott, Foresman, 1901.

Anson, Peter F., *Fisher Folk-Lore: Old Customs, Taboos and Superstitions among Fisher Folk, Especially in Brittany and Normandy, and on the East Coast of Scotland.* London: The Faith Press, 1965.

Apollonius Rhodius, *Argonautica.* Transl. by Edward P. Coleridge. New York: The Heritage Press, 1960.*

Armstrong, Warren, *Sea Phantoms.* New York: The John Day Company, 1961.

Ashton, John, *Curious Creatures in Zoology.* Detroit: Singing Tree Press, 1968 (reprint of 1890 edition).

Bacon, Janet Ruth, *The Voyage of the Argonauts.* Boston: Small, Maynard, 1925.

Baker, Margaret, *Folklore of the Sea.* London: David & Charles, 1979.

Barthell, Edward E., Jr., *Gods and Goddesses of Ancient Greece.* Coral Gables, Florida: University of Miami Press, 1971.

Bascom, Willard, *Deep Water, Ancient Ships.* Garden City, New York: Doubleday, 1976.

Bassett, Fletcher S., *Legends and Superstitions of the Sea and of Sailors, in All Lands and at All Times.* Chicago: Belford, Clarke, 1885.

Beck, Horace, *Folklore and the Sea.* Mystic, Connecticut: The Marine Historical Association, 1979.*

Benwell, Gwen, and Arthur Waugh, *Sea Enchantress: The Tale of the Mermaid and Her Kin.* New York: The Citadel Press, 1965.

Blacker, Carmen, and Michael Loewe, eds., *Ancient Cosmologies.* London: George Allen & Unwin, 1975.

Briggs, Katharine, *An Encyclopedia of Fairies: Hobgoblins, Brownies, Bogies, and Other Supernatural Creatures.* New York: Pantheon Books, 1976.

Bringsværd, Tor Age, *Phantoms and Fairies from Norwegian Folklore.* Transl. by Pat Shaw Iversen. Oslo: Johan Grundt Tanum Forlag, no date.

Brown, Raymond Lamont, *Phantoms of the Sea: Legends, Customs and Superstitions.* New York: Taplinger, 1973.

Bulfinch, Thomas, *Myths of Greece and Rome.* Compiled by Bryan

Holme. New York: Penguin Books, 1981.

Campbell, Joseph, *The Masks of God: Occidental Mythology*. New York: Penguin Books, 1969.

Carrington, Richard, *Mermaids and Mastodons: A Book of Natural & Unnatural History*. New York: Rinehart, 1957.

Casson, Lionel, *The Ancient Mariners: Seafarers and Sea Fighters of the Mediterranean in Ancient Times*. New York: Macmillan, 1959.*

Cavendish, Richard, ed., *Man, Myth & Magic*. 11 vols. New York: Marshall Cavendish, 1983.

Child, Francis James, ed., *The English and Scottish Popular Ballads*. Vol. 1. New York: Pageant, 1956.*

Cole, Joanna, comp., *Best-Loved Folktales of the World*. Garden City, New York: Doubleday, 1982.

Colum, Padraic, *The Golden Fleece and the Heroes Who Lived before Achilles*. New York: Macmillan, 1967.

Craigie, William A., ed. and transl., *Scandinavian Folk-Lore*. Detroit: Singing Tree Press, 1970 (reprint of 1896 edition).

Davidson, H. R. Ellis, *Scandinavian Mythology* (Library of the World's Myths and Legends). London: Hamlyn, 1983.

Davis, F. Hadland, *Myths & Legends of Japan*. New York: Farrar & Rinehart, 1932.*

Deane, Tony, and Tony Shaw, *The Folklore of Cornwall*. Totowa, New Jersey: Rowman and Littlefield, 1975.

De Carli, Franco, *The World of Fish*. Transl. by Jean Richardson. New York: Abbeville Press, 1978.

Dozier, Thomas A., *Dangerous Sea Creatures* (Wild, Wild World of Animals series). New York: Time-Life Films, 1976.

Engel, Leonard, *The Sea* (Life Nature Library). New York: Time Inc., 1961.

Evans, Ivor H., ed., *Brewer's Dictionary of Phrase and Fable*.

New York: Harper & Row, 1970.

Evslin, Bernard, *Greeks Bearing Gifts: The Epics of Achilles and Ulysses*. New York: Four Winds Press, 1971.

Farmer, Penelope, comp. and ed., *Beginnings: Creation Myths of the World*. New York: Atheneum, 1979.

Filby, Frederick A., *The Flood Reconsidered: A Review of the Evidences of Geology, Archaeology, Ancient Literature and the Bible*. London: Pickering & Inglis, 1970.

Frank, Harry Thomas, *Discovering the Biblical World*. Maplewood, New Jersey: Hammond, 1975.

Freund, Philip, *Myths of Creation*. Levittown, New York: Transatlantic Arts, 1975.

Froud, Brian, and Alan Lee, *Faeries*. Ed. by David Larkin. New York: Harry N. Abrams, 1978.*

Gaster, Theodor H., *Myth, Legend, and Custom in the Old Testament*. New York: Harper & Row, 1969.*

Gerhardt, Mia I., *Old Men of the Sea, from Neptunus to Old French Luiton: Ancestry and Character of a Waterspirit*. Amsterdam: Polak & Van Gennep, 1967.

Graham, Winston, *Poldark's Cornwall*. London and Exeter: The Bodley Head and Webb & Bower, 1983.

Grant, Michael, *The Ancient Mediterranean*. New York: Charles Scribner's Sons, 1969.

Graves, Robert, *The Greek Myths*. Vols. 1 and 2. New York: Penguin Books, 1983.*

Gruppe, Henry E., *The Frigates* (The Seafarers series). Alexandria, Virginia: Time-Life Books, 1979.

Guerber, H. A., *Myths of Northern Lands*. Detroit: Singing Tree Press, 1970 (reprint of 1895 edition).

Hadfield, R. L., *The Phantom Ship and Other Ghost Stories of the Sea*. London: Geoffrey Bles, 1937.

Hammond, N.G.L., and H. H.

Scullard, *The Oxford Classical Dictionary*. Oxford, England: The Clarendon Press, 1978.

Hauff, Wilhelm, *The Caravan*. Transl. by Alma Overholt. New York: Thomas Y. Crowell, 1964.*

Homer:
  The Illustrated Odyssey. Transl. by E. V. Rieu. New York: A & W Publishers, 1981.
  The Odyssey of Homer. Transl. by Ennis Rees. New York: The Modern Library, 1960.*

Jensen, Albert C., *Wildlife of the Oceans*. New York: Harry N. Abrams, 1979.

Keightley, Thomas, *The World Guide to Gnomes, Fairies, Elves and Other Little People*. New York: Avenel Books, 1978 (reprint of 1878 edition).

Kemp, Peter, ed., *The Oxford Companion to Ships & the Sea*. London: Oxford University Press, 1976.

Killip, Margaret, *The Folklore of the Isle of Man*. London: B. T. Batsford, 1975.

Knight, Frank, *The Sea Story: Being a Guide to Nautical Reading from Ancient Times to the Close of the Sailing Ship Era*. London: Macmillan, 1958.

Kramer, Samuel Noah, *Cradle of Civilization* (Great Ages of Man series). Alexandria, Virginia: Time-Life Books, 1978.

Krappe, Alexander Haggerty, *Balor with the Evil Eye: Studies in Celtic and French Literature*. New York: Columbia University, 1927.

La Motte-Fouqué, Baron Friedrich de, *Undine*. Transl. by W. L. Courtney. London: William Heinemann, 1925.*

Leach, Maria, ed., *Funk & Wagnalls Standard Dictionary of Folklore, Mythology and Legend*. 2 vols. New York: Funk & Wagnalls, 1949.

Leeming, David, *Mythology*. New York: Newsweek Books, 1977.

Lowry, Shirley Park, *Familiar Mysteries: The Truth in Myths*. New

York: Oxford University Press, 1982.

McCormick, Harold W., and Tom Allen, with Capt. William E. Young, *Shadows in the Sea: The Sharks, Skates and Rays.* Philadelphia: Chilton Books, 1963.

MacCulloch, John Arnott:
The Childhood of Fiction: A Study of Folk Tales and Primitive Thought. London: John Murray, 1905.*
The Mythology of All Races: Eddic. Vol. 2. New York: Cooper Square, 1964.

McGowen, Tom, *Encyclopedia of Legendary Creatures.* Chicago: Rand McNally, 1981.

Mackenzie, Donald A., *Myths of Babylonia and Assyria.* London: Gresham, circa 1930.

Marmur, Mildred, transl., *Japanese Fairy Tales.* New York: Golden Press, 1960.

Marwick, Ernest W., *The Folklore of Orkney and Shetland.* London: B. T. Batsford, 1975.

Mireaux, Emile, *Daily Life in the Time of Homer.* Transl. by Iris Sells. New York: Macmillan, 1965.

Munch, Peter Andreas, *Norse Mythology: Legends of Gods and Heroes.* Transl. by Sigurd Bernhard Hustvedt. New York: AMS Press, 1970 (reprint of 1926 edition).

Ovidius Naso, Publius, *Metamorphoses.* Transl. by Rolfe Humphries. Bloomington, Indiana: Indiana University Press, 1955.

Paré, Ambroise, *On Monsters and Marvels.* Transl. by Janis L. Pallister. Chicago: The University of Chicago Press, 1982.

Phillpotts, Beatrice, *Mermaids.* New York: Ballantine Books, 1980.

Pindarus, *Pindar in English Verse.* Transl. by Arthur S. Way. London: Macmillan, 1922.

The Rand McNally Atlas of the Oceans. New York: Rand McNally, 1977.

Robinson, B. W., *Kuniyoshi: The Warrior-Prints.* Oxford, England: Phaidon, 1982.

Robinson, C. E., *Everyday Life in Ancient Greece.* Oxford, England: The Clarendon Press, 1961.

Sandars, N. K., transl., *The Epic of Gilgamesh.* New York: Penguin Books, 1983.*

Schwab, Gustav, *Gods & Heroes: Myths and Epics of Ancient Greece.* New York: Pantheon Books, 1946.

Seki, Keigo, ed., *Folktales of Japan* (Folktales of the World series). Transl. by Robert J. Adams. Chicago: The University of Chicago Press, 1963.

Simpson, Michael, transl., *Gods and Heroes of the Greeks: The Library of Apollodorus.* Amherst: University of Massachusetts Press, 1976.

Streicher, Sonnfried, *Fabelwesen des Meeres.* Rostock, East Germany: VEB Hinstorff, 1982.

Sturluson, Snorri, *The Prose Edda.* Transl. by Arthur Gilchrist Brodeur. New York: The American Scandinavian Foundation, 1967 (reprint of 1916 edition).

Sweeney, James B., *A Pictorial History of Sea Monsters and Other Dangerous Marine Life.* New York: Crown, 1972.

Thorndike, Joseph J., Jr., ed., *Mysteries of the Deep.* New York: American Heritage, 1980.

Whipple, A. B. C.:
The Clipper Ships (The Seafarers series). Alexandria, Virginia: Time-Life Books, 1980.
The Whalers (The Seafarers series). Alexandria, Virginia: Time-Life Books, 1979.

Whymper, Fred, *The Romance of the Sea: Its Fictions, Facts, and Folk-Lore.* London: Society for Promoting Christian Knowledge, 1896.

* *Titles marked with an asterisk were especially helpful in the preparation of this volume.*

Acknowledgments

The editors wish to thank the following persons and institutions for their help in the preparation of this volume: Ancilla Antonini, Scala, Florence; François Avril, Curator, Département des Manuscrits, Bibliothèque Nationale, Paris; Maria Ceriotti, Marka, Milan; Valerie Chase, National Aquarium, Baltimore; Giancarlo Costa, Milan; Manfred Eger, Richard-Wagner-Museum, Bayreuth; Peter Elze, Worpsweder Archiv, Worpswede, West Germany; Irmgard Ernstmeyer, Hirmer Verlag, Munich; Clark Evans, Rare Book and Special Collections Division, Library of Congress, Washington, D.C.; Marielise Göpel, Archiv für Kunst und Geschichte, West Berlin; Claus Hansmann, Kulturgeschichtliches Archiv, Munich; Christine Hofmann, Bayerische Staatsgemäldesammlungen, Munich; G. Irvine, Department of Oriental Antiquities, British Museum, London; Heidi Klein, Bildarchiv Preussischer Kulturbesitz, West Berlin; Roland Klemig, Bildarchiv Preussischer Kulturbesitz, West Berlin; Tadahiko Kuraishi, Folklore Department, Kokugakuin University, Tokyo; The London Library, London; Margot Ludwig, Richard-Wagner-Museum, Bayreuth; Akiko Moki, Folklore Research Department, Seijo University, Tokyo; Nancy Murphy, Beijing University, China; Rijksmuseum, Amsterdam; B. W. Robinson, London; Justin Schiller, New York City; Robert Shields, Rare Book and Special Collections Division, Library of Congress, Washington, D.C.; Georg Syamken, Kunsthalle, Hamburg.

TIME-LIFE BOOKS

EUROPEAN EDITOR: Kit van Tulleken
Assistant European Editor: Gillian Moore
Design Director: Ed Skyner
Photography Director: Pamela Marke
Chief of Research: Vanessa Kramer
Chief Sub-Editor: Ilse Gray

THE ENCHANTED WORLD

SERIES DIRECTOR: Ellen Phillips
Deputy Editor: Robin Richman
Designer: Dale Pollekoff
Series Administrator: Jane Edwin

Editorial Staff for *Water Spirits*
Text Editors: Tony Allan, Donia Ann Steele
Staff Writer: Stephen G. Hyslop
Researchers: Scarlet Cheng, Trudy Pearson
Assistant Designer: Lorraine D. Rivard
Copy Coordinators: Barbara Fairchild
Quarmby, Robert M. S. Somerville
Picture Coordinator: Nancy C. Scott
Editorial Assistant: Constance B. Strawbridge

Correspondents: Elisabeth Kraemer-Singh
(Bonn); Margot Hapgood, Dorothy Bacon
(London); Miriam Hsia (New York); Maria
Vincenza Aloisi, Josephine du Brusle
(Paris); Ann Natanson (Rome). Valuable
assistance was also provided by:
Janny Hovinga, Wibo van de Linde
(Amsterdam); Jaime A. FlorCruz (Beijing);
Millicent Trowbridge (London); Felix
Rosenthal (Moscow); Christina Lieberman
(New York); Traudl Lessing (Vienna).

Editorial Production
Production Assistants: Nikki Allen, Alan
Godwin, Maureen Kelly
Editorial Department: Theresa John,
Debra Lelliott

ISBN 7054 0890 6

Chief Series Consultant

Tristram Potter Coffin, Professor of
English at the University of Pennsylvania,
is a leading authority on folklore. He is the
author or editor of numerous books and
more than 100 articles. His best-known
works are *The British Traditional Ballad in
North America, The Old Ball Game, The Book of
Christmas Folklore* and *The Female Hero*.

This volume is one of a series that is based
on myths, legends and folk tales.

TIME
LIFE
BOOKS

PRINTED AND BOUND BY BREPOLS S.A.-TURNHOUT, BELGIUM

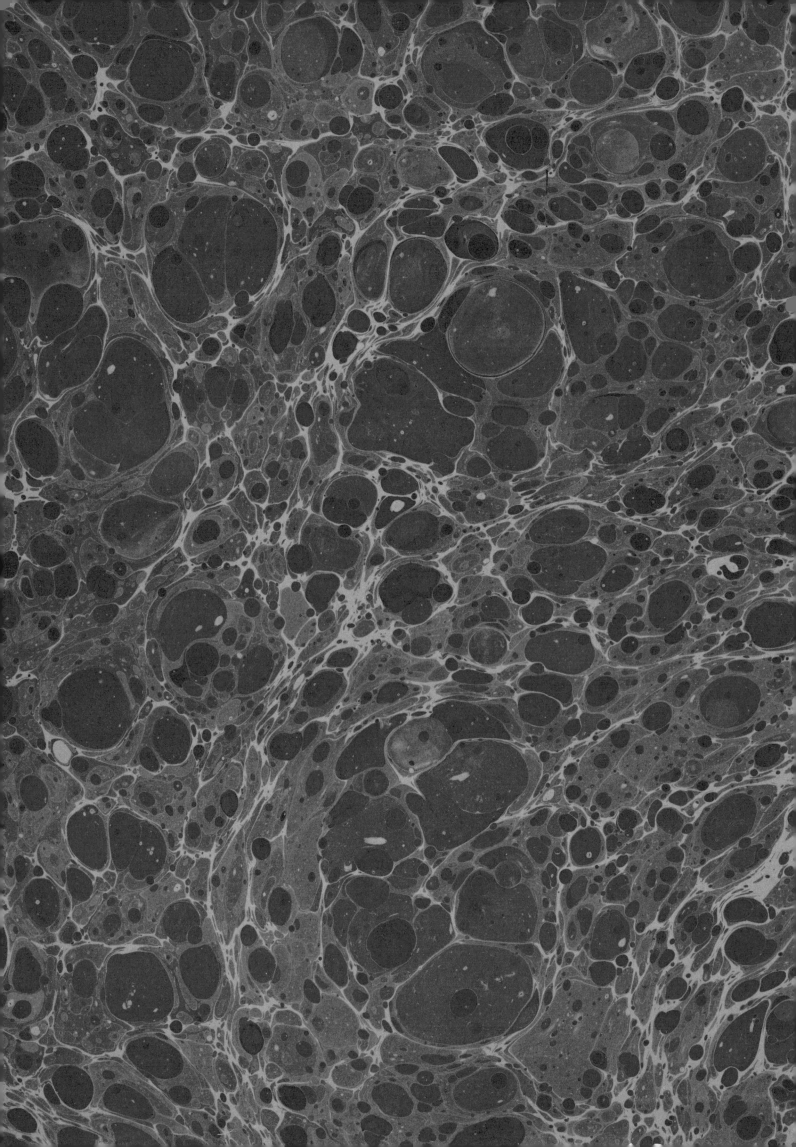